ETERNAL
SUNSHINE

ETERNAL SUNSHINE

LONDRELLE

ISBN: 1544711190
ISBN 13: 9781544711195
Library of Congress Control Number: 2017905115
CreateSpace Independent Publishing Platform
North Charleston, South Carolina

Info@londrelle.com

I offer my respectful
obeisances to God the Mother.
For in love, peace, beauty,
and union, it is She that
we are all seeking.

I offer my respectful
obeisances to God the Father.
For in knowledge, wisdom,
wealth, and power, it is He that
we are all seeking.

It is often that strangers become
family members as a reminder
that we are all God's children.
To a brother and dear friend,
Demetrious "Rious" Williams,
I dedicate this edition to you.

The prophecies may have foretold death,
destruction, and wickedness amongst our kind,
but what is to come is a mass awakening like none other.
The souls of many will transcend into higher dimensions of
thinking, living, and being. You and I will be unified in love,
joy, and harmony. The darkness of illusion will begin to
recede, as heaven enters our hearts and the eternal
bliss of His kingdom lights every corner of our soul.
Eternal, peace, happiness, and sunshine is here.
It is you.

Contents

A little light for those
with the sunflower's soul.

But before we reach light,
we must have first pulled
ourselves out of darkness that
is not reality.

How well do I know these things,
for it was through experience and
suffering that I learned them.

Spirituality & Philosophy

Guiding Light

Life is a maze,
but life is amazing,
and those that learn
to dance in the rain
are more likely to make it.

The puddles of illusion are more
like an oasis, you can choose
to serve God or spend your life
in the matrix.

I leave light in these pages
so that you may find happiness
in your darkest times,
as long as you let yours shine,
heaven isn't hard to find.

We're all divine souls
on a spiritual mission,
to spread love and
positivity in this
physical dimension.

In your search for
happiness you may
fall one-hundred times,
overwhelmed with
pain and traumatized,
but seek ye the kingdom
that is within you,
and you will come to find,
a day as bright as
the summer time.

Sunflowers within you
shall come alive,
when the Seed and
your soul becomes
one inside.

And even in storms
you will come to find,
peace, love, and
eternal sunshine.

Eternal Sunshine

This world may seem a
little cruel and unkind,
but if you believed
in God as much as
you did negativity,
just one time,
I promise you
would experience
eternal sunshine.

You have to learn
to let go of what
you can't control.
Love and master self
to advance your soul.

Dharma

Maybe this life
isn't so much about
trying to achieve our goals,
but rather understanding that
we should embrace what comes
and free what goes.

Whether good or bad, accept all
things as the seasons flow,
realizing that everything you
experience happens only
to feed your soul.

What you consider blessings
might later be lessons that you find,
and all your lessons will be
blessings in due time.

The sun never sets, it's only
you that has moved away,
so if you ever happen
to lose your way,
keep these words in mind
and renew your faith.
Everything will be okay.

Insight

—ɷ—

Maybe this life isn't so much about fulfilling our deepest worldly desires or reaching any fixed destination of personal goals, as much as it is about learning to embrace all of what we have in our current status of life.

Although the latter seems like the obvious choice, we tend to be in constant search of something more. We want to be more than what we are: see more, have more, and experience more. This is understandable, as we come from an infinite source. However, in our quest for abundance, we often become frustrated as we meet misfortune or temporary seasons, where things don't go the way we planned.

Truth be told, it is our labeling of what is fortunate or misfortunate, good or bad, success or failure, which really causes us unnecessary depression and anxiety. Life happens to all of us, regardless of our age or social status and there are things in life that we are destined to experience as both "good" and "bad".

One of the keys to be at peace in this ever-changing life, is to embrace all things as they come, and free them as they go. In doing so, you will find that everything you experience as both "good and bad", comes only with the purpose of helping you grow into the best version of your own self.

The incidents that we may consider to be bad may actually be good in regards to the development of self. Likewise, those things that we consider blessings often turn out to be life lessons in the end.

In all of this, know that God is always with you. We tend to think He has left our side during troubling times, but it may be us who have strayed away.

It is during our darkest days that His light becomes more evident and we realize that He has been there all along, guiding, protecting, and teaching us.

When the storms of life arise and troubles cloud your mind, always remember His promise to never leave or forsake you. Re-affirm your faith and know that everything will be okay. Let peace and love fill your spirit, for God is with you in this hour.

Divine Light

There is nothing in this
world that you can never be,
highs and lows that you
will never see.

Live your life like the
wind and be ever free,
and I guarantee, there
won't be a mountain
top you will never reach.

When heaven speaks,
listen to that voice inside you;
the less you speak and the more
you listen, life will guide you.
And as long as God be with you,
you shall succeed in everything
that you try to.

Every moment that you
exist feel blessed today,
worry about tomorrow yesterday.
To be free is knowing that the
universe speaks within
every breath you take.

Even if you fall once,
be sure to climb twice.
Times will get dark,
but you shine bright.
You are. Divine Light.

Insight

—⁓—

As the saying goes, if you can dream it, you can achieve it. We live in a world of endless possibilities and potential. Miracles are literally taking place in every moment of our lives. All of our hopes, dreams, and aspirations are just a progressive thought away from becoming reality, catapulting us into newfound success and happiness.

However, because we are bound by the laws of nature and are governed by a stringent of universal laws, we are destined to experience both the positive and the negative aspects of our world.

Without pain or sorrow, it wouldn't be possible for us to know what it feels like to be truly happy. Without the experience of failure, it's likely that we wouldn't appreciate success. Without going through heart breaking situations, we wouldn't be able to recognize and value true love.

It is within this simple truth that a glimpse of what is likely to come can be found and, as we analyze our lives, we can see that life is much like a roller coaster, taking us on a journey of highs, lows, twists, turns, and sometimes completely flipping us upside down.

All of this is not for the sake of mere experience, but to groom us into what we are to become. The lows are just as important as the highs in life, and maybe even more exciting, for it is here that the mystery of our lives is being written and anticipation builds, as we climb the ladder of personal growth. The lows provide us with humbling experiences that help ground and nurture our spirit so that we may rise to unimaginable highs.

The tree is the tallest living organism on the planet, but its massive height would not be reached if it were not first firmly planted, rooted, and grounded in Mother Earth. Like trees, it is imperative that we too, be grounded in our nature and deeply rooted in our faith if we wish to grow upwards in success.

Nothing in life happens by coincidence; you are where you are because it's where you need to be to continue your evolution and fulfill your personal destiny. There are powers far greater than what you may comprehend that are aiding you in this process, and you must learn to trust in these powers.

These powers are very subtle, much like the gentle breeze that gracefully guides the sailboat at sea; an unseen force is always present in our lives. Most of us go through life not realizing this. But, the moment we do, we will be able to live and embrace life freely, knowing that we are not alone as we cross this ocean of life.

To live like the wind means allowing yourself to go with the flow of life, not necessarily care-less, but care-free. So much anxiety is caused by our worrying about the past and about tomorrow, none of which we have control over.

Every moment of every day should be lived and embraced with every second that goes by. It is when we live in the "here" and "now" that we are able to see how much God has blessed us with and how abundant life truly is.

The "here" and "now" is where dreams can be manifested and the spirit of life can be felt. It is only when you are focused on the "here" and "now" that you can hear and receive the wisdom of the universe.

The "here" and "now" is neither influenced by the past nor fixated on the future. Rather, it is every bit of eternity existing at this moment and, as you read these lines, you are slowly being engulfed into and taken away by the waves of its presence. The "here" and "now" is now, and it is the only time that matters!

When we are not living in the "here" and "now", life can be a drag. We count the days and weeks as they go by, wishing for the future and holding on to things from our past.

Holding on to what has happened to us in the past is much like carrying a bag full of bricks and complaining about how much it's weighing us down. The more intelligent thing to do is to simply take the bag off our shoulders and continue walking our path, though many people do not believe it to be this simple.

Even though we should always have goals and a clear direction for the future, we shouldn't worry so much about how we are going to get there. If we focus on what we want to achieve and where we wish to go, the universe will make sure to guide us there, just like a GPS.

For some, that guidance will come through God; others believe it will come through a higher sense of self, or that it will be delivered by that voice within us. No matter what name we give to our own GPS, we must learn to listen to it and to trust its guidance and direction.

By accepting and embracing this guidance, we will come to understand that life has truly been working in our favor.

We were created in the spirit of love; everything we are and ever will be *is* love. It is our natural state of being. Darkness will never overcome the light of love and nothing you endure will ever break the eternal bond you have with the creator.

You are divine light, traveling through time and space on a divine mission. Let the light of your spirit shine through.

Bright Side

Somedays it may be
hard to look at life
on the bright side,
especially when your
darkest hours arise
at mid-day instead
of night time,
and all of your hope
seems to melt away
like candles when
the light dies.

But rest assure,
everything will
be quite fine.
It is darkness alone
that influences us
to let our light shine.

You and I live for the
same reasons that
Jesus Christ died,
to sing the glories
of heaven in each
and every lifetime.

In tight times you may
pray for days and nights,
but as long as you place
your faith in God and
not thy faith in sight,
even your darkest days
will be replaced with light.

Make A Way

Even though it
may seem like
you're just living
day to day,
trouble doesn't
last always,
I promise you
heaven will
make a way.

Try not to worry
so much about
the future and
embrace today.
Every atom that
you breathe is
filled with
amazing grace.

In every mirror
that you see,
you're starring
at a miracle
face to face,
if you would
only exercise
your faith all
of your worries
will be chased
away.

It's safe to say
that life is only
a graceful race,
simply take your time
and you'll be fine.
I promise you,
heaven will
make a way.

Sunflowers & Sunshine

Life can't be all
sunflowers and sunshine,
in order for you to grow
you have to experience
the rain sometimes.

You're no different from
the flowers and nature,
so just give thanks to the creator,
as he blesses you with the power
to make it, through any situation.

Everything happens for a reason
and life tends to flow in seasons,
so whether your faith is in
the Buddha or Christ Jesus,
there's always an angel there
to help you conquer your demons,
when you really need it.

Insight

—〰—

S ince as far as I can remember, I've always been fascinated by sunflowers. Their elegant petals and radiant core have had a way of inducing great amounts of peace, clarity, and bliss upon my being.

The same is true with the bright and captivating sun, as it has always inspired happiness within me. When we close our eyes and picture the two together, what we envision enchants our imagination. Happy, fun, joyful, and peaceful may all be words that come to mind as we drift into this dream world.

However, as much as we would like to spend the rest of our days in this euphoric paradise, the laws of nature prove this to be short-lived and nearly impossible. The sun must set, flowers wither away as seasons change, and rain too must come in order for Mother Nature to manifest her beauty once again.

Though possessing the highest level of consciousness amongst living things on this planet, we also are subjected to these laws of nature; in fact, we are not different from the flowers and nature. For us, rain can come in the form of misfortune, tragic events, or accidents; we may be hurt by someone, we may have lost love, or we may be faced with the loss of loved ones.

Contrary to what most of us would like to believe, all of these events are essential to our growth. For without any of them we wouldn't be able to progress spiritually or emotionally in life. There's something about problems and difficulties that bring out the best in us, as they force us to focus on what really matters and remind us to stay ever dependent on the mercy of God.

During these trying times, we must be like flowers and stand firm in our "nature" or, in this case, our faith, and allow the rain to pass. We must give thanks in the midst of our "storm" because it is by grace alone that the storm has come and it is only by grace that we will be given the strength to endure and overcome. It is only after the waters have receded and the clouds have vanished, that we understand the meaning and purpose behind the natural disasters that happen in our life.

Sure enough, there is no escaping certain miseries in this world, but it's important to know that all things come and go as the seasons, for proper reasons. Learn to dance in the rain, celebrate new beginnings, and embrace troubling times, as all things come with the purpose of allowing us to develop into a better and stronger version of ourselves.

Lucidness

In order to be happy
in life you have to
learn to let the pain go,
some people never get
to see the beauty of a
rainbow, because they
have yet to let the rain go.

You have to stop feeling
sorry for yourself,
living in misery,
and stop giving all your
time and energy to
negativity.

Insight

—⟋⟍—

The many seasons of life are inevitable. It is only those who are able to recognize this simple truth and maintain an optimistic view of the future, that make it through these ever changing times.

Contrastingly, there may be others who can't see the lessons that need to be learned when rainy and harsh seasons come into their lives. These individuals fail to adapt to the changing conditions and they never grow from these situations. Instead, they hold on to them, even after the season or storm has passed, and they inflict further pain on themselves by allowing negative thoughts and emotions to occupy their mind, time, and consume their energy.

Though it must rain, it's important that we do not hold on to the mess it may have caused in our lives. For when we do, we carry this mess with us and we are likely to become the mess ourselves. Becoming a mess can cause instability and chaos in different areas of our lives. We may begin to have issues at work, school, in our friendships, or in our relationships with family members and significant others. The longer we allow the storms of our past to occupy our minds, the more disruption they will bring, preventing us from moving forward in life.

They key is to let go. Unfortunately, there is no explainable method to do so, as sometimes it is not as simple as it sounds. Or maybe it is, when things are heavy, do you not put them down? The problem is that we want to rationalize and reason with our troubles. We try to think of things we could have done to prevent them from occurring, or search for reasons why they have chosen to wreak havoc on our lives specifically. In doing so, we only delay the process of letting go and allow the storms of negativity to shower us with sorrow, depression, and pain.

When we let go, we detach ourselves from the things that are causing us unnecessary stress. We often hold on to past seasons because there is an object or thing that we are still attached to and we want to hold on to every bit of it, even if it hurts us. This is the underlying cause of our not wanting to let go and the reason why we make excuses for not being able to or not knowing how to let go. It may be something material that we worked hard for that was lost in the storm and we don't want to part with the thought of not having it anymore. It may also be a person who has become the source of the storms in our lives or who was a part of a larger storm. This is the more difficult of the two to accept, but it can be solved in the same simplistic way: if they are heavy, put them down.

Like all things, letting go is a learning process; you have to go through it to master the art of doing so. As you learn more and more of how simple it is to let go, you will welcome and appreciate all the storms that come into your life, for you have the understanding that the season is only temporary and necessary for your growth and development.

In order for us to receive greater and better, we must first be willing to release the things that no longer have a progressive purpose in our lives. Don't be an emotional hoarder; make room in your heart and mind for better things to manifest and grow. In nature, the rainbow is a symbol that God has finished Her work and we can now look forward to a brighter day as the sun begins to peak through the clouds and the water recedes.

She is the messenger of love from a loving God; with her awe-inspiring colors, she reminds us that this too shall pass, and the result of these storms will be of beauty, prosperity, and new beginnings. Claim your new fresh start, celebrate with joy and excitement. You have endured yet another storm and have allowed growth to take place within your heart. Abundance is yours!

Motions

No matter what you face
in life you have to always
think in a progressive way,
regardless of how many
times you fall, your strength,
you should never underestimate,   *resilience*
you can and will overcome
your depressive states.

Life is only a roller coaster
of emotions and tested faith,
if you can find a way to
celebrate the highs and lows
you can live peaceful
in this blessed place.

Be free from the pain of
your past and let go of
all the extra weight, ∴ *stop fighting quicksand*
learn to dance with life
with grace at a steady pace,
not too fast and not too slow,
happiness is just a breath away.

Insight

—⚮—

Some of us live our entire lives dealing with depression, never reaching in and pulling ourselves out of the graves of our own thoughts. Many doctors and psychiatrists may label depression as a disorder or a disease, often prescribing anti-depressants that rarely help their patients overcome the problem.

However, depression is not a disease or a disorder; it is a state of mind and, like all states of mind, it can be changed. The first of many steps in changing your state of mind is changing what you consume in regards to your senses. We use our five senses as a way of perceiving the outer world and to receive knowledge.

If through our senses we are perceiving and consuming toxic things, then we subject our inner world to be influenced by these things. Changing the things we read, watch, eat, listen to, and the people we associate with, will play a major role in the development of a more positive and progressive attitude.

The mind is a sort of database. Within it, it has stored an incalculable number of thoughts that accumulate over the duration of one's life. Some are positive and some are negative. Usually, a person who deals with depression has mountains of negative thoughts, emotions, and memories stored in their database. This may be due to personal experiences, hurtful things people have said to them, or messages they gather from music, reading, or even social media. All of these things make impressions on our minds and influence its state.

In order for us to overcome these negative thoughts, we have to reinforce our minds with positive thoughts and experiences. Anytime a negative thought arises, immediately speak or write down a positive affirmation. This is one simple way of changing your state of mind. Over time, with constant practice, you will see a noticeable difference in how you react to and are affected by negative thoughts.

It will also do you some justice to ask yourself daily, "What am I feeding myself?" We not only feed our being through our mouths, but also through our eyes, ears, nose, and touch as well. As mentioned before, it is through our senses that we perceive and experience the world. Every day we must "arm and protect" ourselves for what we are about to perceive and experience.

When we arm ourselves appropriately, we are less likely to allow depression and stress to find their way into our minds or affect us in the worst way. Most of us have the habit of waking with just enough time to make it to work, school, or wherever we may have to be at a specific time. We give ourselves no time to prepare mentally, physically, or spiritually for our day, thus leaving us vulnerable to things that may affect us negatively.

It's acceptable to have a few bad days here and there, but for one who is constantly having bad days, this may be a sign that they are not feeding themselves the best of things. Again, this is not referring to ingesting food, but to metaphorically feeding our senses.

If the eyes are the windows to the soul, do not read impure things, for they will surely stain and break the glass that leads to your heart and mind, letting contaminated things inside. As you wake up and go about your day, read positive messages and inspiring quotes, or watch uplifting programs. If you have the habit of checking your social media every morning, be sure to avoid gossipy or profane content as these things negatively affect your subconscious mind and are much like trash added to your database of thoughts.

We think and repeat what we hear. Therefore, divert yourself from listening to messages that are not progressive and uplifting to your inner spirit. When you listen to explicit music or commentary, you consume these things, repeat these things, and help manifest them in your reality.

 Eating healthy and nutritional food also results in having a better mood and healthier emotions. There are proven connections between unhealthy food and negative emotions and we have to remember that it is through eating that we are being energized, as food is our fuel. Fueling up on unhealthy things will not allow us longevity in life or throughout our daily routines. Healthy food helps produce a healthy mind and a brighter sprit. If you eat things that make you feel lighter and more energized, you will see clear changes in your mood and emotions.

More important than protecting our mind and body against unhealthy things, is our need to protect our spirit-soul against these things as well.

The body is to be known as the city of nine gates (two eyes, two ears, two nostrils, one mouth, anus, and genitalia). Within these gates resides the soul and, due to the impure things that we allow into our kingdom via our senses and through these gates, the pure spirit-soul becomes negatively conditioned by these impurities.

Naturally, the soul is free and untouched, but because we are in contact with this material (physical) nature, it is subject to being placed under illusion and affected by the things we give our energy to. The prescribed method for liberating and freeing the soul from such illusion, is the chanting of the name of God.

As a follower and practitioner of this method, I myself can say that this method alone has relieved me from my darkest days of depression and made me a more joyful, happier, and blissful being. Beyond this, the method has awakened my spiritual nature and revived my God consciousness, which is the ultimate aim of human life. The chanting of the names of God lessens and purifies the negative impressions made upon our minds by things that are impure. God is one, but His are names many, there is power is His name.

As we look deep into the causes of depression, we will come to find that the source of all depression is centered around things that are material. Our bodies, our possessions, our wants and desires, all material things, are cause for much of the anxiety and emotional stress we encounter. This material world is a temporary manifestation of God's creation and, if we continue to allow material things to be the source of our happiness, we will continue to experience temporary happiness.

It is only when we elevate ourselves to the spiritual platform, that we finally experience eternal sunshine, eternal happiness, and eternal bliss. The sprit-soul is eternal, full of knowledge and bliss, but when we are not elevated to any sort of spiritual consciousness, we become ego-driven souls, interested only in material gain and in satisfying our senses. Driven by the illusions of our mind and bodies, we think that our material possessions, wants, and desires are what will make us happy, only to find this to be false. These false conceptions lead us into depression and are the source of our anxiety.

You are spirit-soul: until you return back to your spiritual nature, you will always be under much stress and anxiety. What you are searching for is eternity: the only two things you will experience in this temporary manifestation that are of this nature, is you and God.

Let this be the source of your happiness and you will, without a doubt, put an end to all of your depression and unnecessary anxiety. The closer you get to God and revert back to your natural state of eternal consciousness, the more you will recognize that all of this human experience is a test of your faith and of your ability to trust in the unseen. Everything you will ever endure or encounter, will happen only to help you realize your spiritual nature, to awaken you to the reality that is in the unseen.

You are sprit-soul, you are eternal, and your happiness will only come from things of this nature. This bliss that fills my spirit, as I share these findings with you, is incomparable to any material feeling that can be described in human language.

It is in these truths that I have found the eternal sunshine that is hidden within the darkness of depression, anxiety, and stress. I am you and you are me. We are reflections of each other; you too can overcome any obstacle you face by writing the above mentioned poem on the windows of your heart.

Life is only a roller coaster of emotions and tested faith, if you can find a way to celebrate the highs and lows, you can live peaceful in this blessed place. This is the essence of this piece. Even when we are elevated to spiritual consciousness, there will still be obstacles and tests to overcome, but they will be more obvious as we become more aware of the nature of this human experience.

Furthering on our path, we learn to be equipoised in both the highs and lows we encounter on our journey back home. We live this life in celebration, for it is a gift that we have received from the Divine Mother. She is the nurturer and loving mother of all who have taken birth in this plane of existence.

As we attain God consciousness, which is the goal of human life, much of what we once believed to be horrific and unbearable, becomes a poetic expression of hurt, pain, failure, depression, love, happiness, and triumph.

This is the beauty that we call life. It is to be danced with in such a way that we are eager to meet every day in a spirit of love and excitement, for we know that we are here to learn and experience something that will take our breath away. Every day, happiness is just a breath away.

Elevation

Sometimes the hurt
is so deep it feels like
you're allergic to life.

And things seem to only
get worse every day,
it's like you're cursed,
but you still search
to find your purpose in life.

Having suicidal revelations
overdosing on drugs
and medication.

I just want you to know
that every test you're facing
is preparation for your elevation.

Blessings

Times may get hard,
don't spend all your days
interacting with stress.
Just be thankful for
your position because
there are some that are
happier with less.

God is the perfect teacher,
don't dismiss his lessons.
Those that are patient
in their situation
always get the blessings.

Insight

—ɯ—

Tough times happen to all of us, whether we are having financial trouble, relationship problems, issues in school, or just an overall bad day. During these times, it may be hard to look on the bright side, especially when things aren't going as expected. However, I find by way of experience that, within our struggles, there are hidden blessings and messages that come disguised as misfortune.

Many times, it takes misfortune to redirect us back onto our destiny and, though it may be very painful or depressing while treading these pathways, things always seem to work out for the better. It doesn't matter what the perceived problem may be; all that matters is how we handle it, what definition we give it, and whether or not we allow it to build us or break us.

Worrying about your problems only magnifies the issue and attracts more problems into your life, often spreading to different areas as well. Your worries and thoughts only have the power that you give them. When they enter your mind, immediately divert your thoughts to something progressive and positive.

It's also good to vocalize your releasing of these detrimental thoughts by way of affirmation such as, "I release all harmful and toxic thoughts from my mind at this moment" or, "I no longer give these thoughts the power to hurt me or negatively affect my life."

During these tough times, our focus should not be to remove challenges from our life, but to explore ways to maximize our misfortune. Analyze your current situation, meditate on things you could improve on within yourself, and use this as an opportunity to manifest a positive change in your life.

It's usually during times of chaos that we really start to focus on life. When things are really going bad, we realize it's time to buckle up and get ourselves together to prevent us from falling any more than we already have.

It is also during times of chaos that we seek and realize the presence of God. Our feelings of helplessness and/or hurt bring us into a state of need to believe in something higher than ourselves and call upon His name. God is a master teacher and He will never place a burden on us that is too much for us to bear. The tests you are currently facing are not punishment for something you've done, but are simply conditioning you for all the blessings that you will one day receive.

All too often we get caught up in our losses and dismiss some of God's quiet gifts, taking for granted the little things that go unnoticed in our daily lives. Things like fresh water, family, nature, or sunlight are all gifts from our Divine creator. Whenever we feel the need to complain about what we don't have, we should stop before completing the idea and give instant gratitude for what we do have. You'd be amazed at how this simple gesture will attract great things into your life.

Whatever your struggle or hardship may be, understand that your greatness is only as great as our test. If you plan on being great in life, you have to accept the lessons that come with greatness. There are things you won't have time to learn once you have reached your goal. Hence, it is best that you learn them while in the process of reaching your destination. Have patience and know that the Divine is always with you. Continue to reaffirm yourself and your faith and ask for guidance. All things are working in your favor.

Self-Destruction

Sometimes we keep
memories of hurt and
heart-break buried
so deep inside,
they begin to eat alive,
and destroy our
peace of mind.

We become prisoners
of our own thoughts,
crucified and nailed
to our own cross.

All we can do is pray
and lean on God
to help us up
before we eventually
self-destruct.

Insight

—⚋—

The memories of things or people that have hurt us in the past can put us in a deeply depressing state of mind. One thought can trigger a "play-by-play" reenactment of the event in our minds and haunt us for as long as we allow it.

Those same events, even though they may have happened months or even years ago, plague us and chain us mentally, with seemingly no way of escaping. It may be hard to tell people about these things, because we have kept them buried deep inside our hearts for so long, and to bring them up would be self-torture or near suicide. One of the worst things you can do in these situations is to keep your feelings and emotions bottled up inside of you. Doing this is a sure way to drive yourself deeper into depression and self-hurt.

Holding on to harmful thoughts allows them to hurt you even more. Although they are not actually happening at the current moment, they still eat away at your spirit and sometimes only make matters worse. If you don't have a close friend or family member you feel comfortable speaking with about these issues, I suggest purchasing a notebook or composition book and journaling your thoughts. I know it may seem a little outdated in this day and age, but I have kept one myself over the last two years and it's amazing to go back and read some of my entries, seeing the mental battles I've overcome.

It is also imperative that we learn to practice forgiveness if we would like to dispel the darkness of our past. When we forgive the things and people that have hurt us we no longer allow them to continue to affect our state of mind in the present moment. Not only is it important to forgive others, but we must also learn to forgive ourselves as well. Sometimes we can be the cause of our own inner turmoil because we haven't reconciled with our own mistakes and accepted our wrong doings. Though it may be tough, you must understand that you have to live with you for the rest of your life, forgive so that you may open new doors and opportunities to replace the memories of old. There is great power in your forgiveness, in that you mentally and emotionally free yourself from the bondage of past events and allow the spirit of love to grow and heal all that you have endured. In forgiveness there is freedom, a freedom that allows you experience life and love again, freely.

I can attest that no matter how mentally strong you may be, there are some things you won't be able to handle in life. It is during trying times that we must rely not on our own mental toughness, but on the salvation and shelter of God. As someone who has overcome many unfortunate events in life,

I can tell you the only sure way to rid yourself of these nightmares is to pray.

Prayer works wonders in our lives, as it's a direct access to the divine creator and absolute power, which has the ability to instantly heal all of our troubles. I remember a Bible verse that a college friend of mine would recite to lift me up during troubling times. It states, "Let us therefore come boldly to the throne of grace, that we may obtain mercy and find grace to help in the time of need."

Prayer is your greatest resource. There is a God, and He is waiting with open arms to assist you in all of your battles.

Paradise

No one ever said it
didn't rain in paradise,
though it may bring
hurricanes of pain,
you have to be thankful
that you even have life.

The mind can be a parasite
leaving you with feelings
of depression and defeat,
or the mind can be your
friend leaving humble
blessings at your feet.

It's all about how
you see things in the
perception that you think.
Always embrace life
with love regardless
of the lessons that
you reach.

This message that I leave
is worth more than
diamond gems,
as long as you keep
your eyes on God
the sun will shine again.

Time and time again
He has tested your faith,
as long as you keep your
eyes on God, the sun will
shine for the rest of your days.

Insight

—〰—

A bove body, there is mind. And above mind, there is spirit, soul. When individuals are in the bodily conception of life, they believe themselves to be body, regarding themselves as Black/African American, Italian, Spanish, or belonging to a particular land.

When people believe they are the mind, relying on intelligence alone, they operate completely on the mental level, placing their faith into the vast majority of universal laws.

When people reach the spiritual platform of knowledge and intelligence, they come to the realization that "I am neither the body nor the mind, but I am spirit soul." The mind and body are subordinate to the soul and should in all instances be sub-servant to it. However, as we experience in our everyday lives, this is not always the case.

The mind tends to wander aimlessly and if we are not careful at monitoring it, it can drive us deep into depressing or detrimental thoughts. For us, the mind can be the cause of bondage or the giver of freedom and it is for this reason it must be tamed. The mind can either bring you blessings or it can be the deliverer of pain. It is pivotal that you train your mind in such a way that you reject all negative thoughts and influences as they arise.

A person with a trained mind, even when faced with difficulty in life, is able to rise above misfortune and depression. This is due to his or her ability to focus their mind on more positive and progressive thoughts when negativity enters their life. From personal experience, I can attest that this is no easy feat to overcome and it was only after many years of trial and error that I found a method that worked for me.

This method was meditation. The chief aim of all systems of yoga and meditation is to train the mind, drawing it from the material and fixing it on the spiritual, on God. The majority of my mental suffering was due to material wants and desires. It was only when I began to transcend these desires, replacing them with the desire to know and love God, that I was able to climb out of the graves of depression. God should be the center of our lives and the focus of all meditative practices.

When we take to this approach, our worries become less and all areas of life begin to grow accordingly. This can be compared to the growing of a tree. God is the root and foundation of all things. When we water and nurture this root, the tree begins to bear fruit, or in our case, success, happiness, and abundance.

When we make the source of our happiness material things, we make ourselves vulnerable to depression, anxiety, and hurt. These things are temporary; they come and go as the seasons change.

God is eternal and you are eternal. Place the source of your happiness in the eternal. The only sure way to end the inevitable suffering of life is to come to this point, switching your focus on the Divine. As Lord Krishna states in the Bhagavad Gita, "One must deliver himself with the help of his mind, and not degrade himself, for the mind can be both a friend and an enemy".

Inner Peace

Waste not all of your
days and nights trying
to figure out what's
wrong and what's right.
Although the mind and
heart must fight,
you have to learn to
be still and trust life.

Be not so uptight,
expecting things to
happen instantly,
if it happens then its
meant to be, all things
come together eventually.

Walk like waves on the
ocean to the beat of
your own symphony,
let the seas of emotions
carry you only with
compassion and empathy,
and love shine through
your eyes with the
energy of sympathy.

Be at one, synergy, with
all things that have life,
giving thanks and gratitude
to whatever name you call
Christ, every morning
and last night.

May every word that I
speak give you strength
when you are feeling weak,
these words that I leave,
are all you need on the path
to inner peace.

Insight

—⚶—

T he secret to finding peace and happiness is realizing that it can be found exactly where you are today. It exist not on some remote island or tropical paradise. Nor does it linger in the past or await you in the future, but the peace you seek is gently calling you from where you stand now. Within your very own being, in the stillness of silence and solitude, there exist a fountain of joy and bliss. Rest on the banks of your mind and drink of the rivers of your own soul. You are the peace you seek.

Dreams

Every time that it seems
like life is punishing you,
understand that you're only
being prepared for everything
that you have coming to you.
Your hopes and aspirations
may not have manifested
when you wanted them to,
but the universe is working
to make every one of them true.

Trust and believe and
you shall receive.
This has been God's
eternal promise since
Adam and Eve.
We all have dreams
of extravagant things,
but a tree must first grow
before you gather its leaves,
and winter must come
to balance the spring,
and flowers do die in
the palace of queens.

All that matters with dreams
is that you keep them alive,
have faith in yourself
defeating demons inside.
All that matters with dreams
is that you keep them alive,
This is your God-given purpose,
and your reason to fly.

Insight

—〰—

Call it God, universe, or by any other name; they are all synonyms and whichever one you choose to use will be fair and just. Prayer and the laws of attraction are also synonymous and backed by the fact that if you truly want it with all of your heart, it shall be given unto you.

One of the factors we forget when applying the laws of attraction to our lives and while we are in prayer, is the concept of time. The universe does not operate on the basis of time. Rather, it is free from all concepts of it, and it breaks all rules concerning it. This is why there are occasions in which you may pray for a certain thing and it may come immediately and conversely, while other times you may ask diligently for something and its arrival is delayed or does not come at all.

Do not let time discourage you from pursuing your dreams and, most importantly, do not let it disrupt you from praying. Though you may have been waiting for days, months, or even years for your dreams to be fulfilled, this has only been a moment in the spiritual realm.

"It will happen in a moment, in the blink of an eye, when the last trumpet is blown. For when the trumpet sounds, those who have died will be raised to live forever. And we who are living will also be transformed."

Let these words fill and uplift your spirit when you feel weary due to the illusion of time. Miracles do happen in the blink of an eye and dreams can come true without a second's notice. The person who truly believes within his mind and heart, awakens the soul of the universe, summoning it to deliver in full what he has requested of it.

There are three ways one can wait while they are being prepared for their dreams to come true. The first is waiting with worry. The person who waits in this manner believes that life is punishing them, disallowing them to reach and attain their goals. The individual waits with much anxiety, helplessly hoping for the day that life releases them from its grip and delivers success. By waiting in this manner, a person tends to gradually lose faith in the goals he or she has set and will ultimately never achieve them.

The second method is waiting passively. Waiting in this way, one usually goes day to day with a care-free attitude toward their dreams. The attitude here is, "if it happens, it happens." While this is a subtle and more acceptable approach, it is not the best of methods.

The third and final way to wait is with enthusiasm. The person who waits with enthusiasm is excited about the forthcoming of their blessings, so much so that they can see and feel themselves already living their dreams. They give constant gratitude to the universe for preparing them to receive everything that they are about to receive, because they are indeed ready to have it.

The universe responds to emotions. Emotions of love, appreciation, and enthusiasm effectively and positively communicate with the intelligence of the universe, bringing your dreams that much closer to fulfillment.

Be excited about your dreams, hopes, and aspirations. Live every day in anticipation knowing that your blessing is coming and celebrate with gratitude, as if you already have it. Your dreams are yours for a reason. They are tied to your purpose in this world, and lead you on your path to eternal sunshine. When God says it's your time, nobody and nothing can say otherwise: you have proven yourself worthy.

When Destiny Calls

There will be days
that you have to
sacrifice your time
for the things that
you need the most.

And anyone who
doesn't add value
to your life, you
will have to learn to
let these people go,
if you ever want
to reach your goals.

These are things that
you need to know
in order for your
seed to grow.

A flower never
blooms if it holds
on the weeds below.
When destiny calls,
you have to learn
to let people go.

Insight

—ɷ—

D estiny is such a beautiful thing and it is unfolding every second of every moment in our lives. From the moment of our physical birth, we are, with the help of the divine spirit, writing and living out our destiny. Each and every one of us has a personal destiny or life mission that has been given to us before we accepted a body and took birth in this material world.

Our destiny in this lifetime is in direct association with our karma from lives past, and each individual soul has incarnated as a result of the actions and reactions of previous births. Just like a cruise ship never aimlessly sails into the ocean, and a flight rarely takes off without knowing its destination, we are not here for the sake of being here, going nowhere or having no purpose.

If there is life here, there must have been life before and there will be life beyond. This is a place of development in which we prepare ourselves for our ultimate destiny. Back to Godhead.

Though God has granted us limited free will, destiny is nothing we completely control or manipulate. It is written, Maktub, as expressed in Paul Coelho's "The Alchemist." You cannot escape your destiny but you can, as you may have experienced in your own life, prolong it. Though the paths to your destiny are many, it is prolonged when we believe ourselves to be the master of it and try to force or speed up the process in fulfilling it.

Usually, when doing so, we become frustrated because nothing seems to be going our way or it almost seems as though life is against us. We then lose focus of all of our goals or even adapt new ones that are not in accordance with our purpose in life. When life seems like it's against you or you are met with a ton of resistance that eats away at your spirit, making you feel weak, lazy, or as if you have no purpose in it, you are almost always going against your destiny. It's not that life is against you, but rather you are going against it, and it's trying to get you back on your life path. The only surefire way for it to do so is by showing you the opposite of what you wish to experience–Pain.

This pain we experience influences us to reevaluate our lives, goals, relationships, career choices and, if we are wise, ultimately it will influence us to turn our lives around and head in the right direction. Though it is written, your destiny is not something you would be unhappy fulfilling or enjoy reaching. In fact, it is aligned with your very nature. All of your talents, gifts, interests, and abilities are in direct accordance with your life's purpose and ultimately, your destiny.

A life of unfullfilment leads to an unfulfilled destiny. In order for us to be fulfilled in this life we must embrace who we are and what we are capable of achieving. As already mentioned, your gifts and talents are a part of your life's mission, they are the vehicles that take you to your life's destination and keys that are used to open the gates of your destiny.

Talents and gifts are not acquired; they are only given by grace. All of us were born with a unique set of gifts that are essential to our purpose in life, and as such, they must be embraced and used for the total fulfillment of our being. No person's talents are greater than another's and no man's destiny is greater than the next, for we are all eternal servants of God and we are here to use what we've been blessed with to worship and serve Him. It is only when you are using your gifts and abilities in service to God that your life becomes more fulfilling and your destiny becomes more evident as you move towards it.

When you are finally walking towards and aware of your destiny, there will be an overwhelming feeling of joy and bliss that fills your spirit. It will feel like "home" in the sense that everything that you're good at will come natural to you and if you do these things for a living it won't feel like "work" at all.

This is how you know for sure that you are entering into your life's purpose. Blessings and new opportunities will come from places near and far, and others will compliment you, telling you how (whatever it is that you do) has affected their lives in a positive way.

It's truly a great feeling, but there is a price to pay when you answer the call of your destiny. Though the destination may become more clear, the mountains you will have to climb will not cease to appear. This is in no way done to discourage you from continuing on the path of your destiny, but to remind you that reaching your destiny is a lifelong journey, and it is completed only when you depart this world.

There is much to be written and learned in between the "once upon a time" and "the end" of your story, so be patient and embrace all that you are presented with as your story is being written. Like any great novel or movie, there will be plot twists, rising actions, climaxes, falling actions, antagonists, etc., so be attentive and aware of the drama of your story.

The drama of your life is one of the aspects within your destiny that you have a substantial amount of control over. It's limited, but fair. We can't play all the roles in our life's story and others are needed to help us advance on this path. We are entitled to have parents, siblings, family members, and a host of others that play a significant role in who we are to become.

Then, there is the role of the significant other or the object of our love and affection, and this is where the drama begins and the story starts to become interesting. Nothing happens by chance and those who have the roles of being your lover are not given the chance to do so at random.

More than your parents and teachers, these people mean the most to your destiny. Love is our driving force in life, our reason for living, and we are in constant search for it.

Hence, love plays a pivotal part in whether we fulfill our destiny or not. Love and destiny go hand in hand, but the problem arises when we try to extend the roles of people who are only meant to make a small appearance in our life's story. As you begin to live out your destiny, you will know who these people are, and they will no longer fit the storyline or theme your life. Out of your love for what once was, you will try to write them in your story but, over time, they will prove that they can't live up to the part you're trying to give them. The more you resist moving on from this chapter of your life, the more time passes by and your quest of reaching your destiny is prolonged.

More painful than going in the opposite direction of your destiny, is knowing which way you need to go, but holding on to something that cannot go where you're going. Though some people play major roles in the story of our lives, they are not periods, but rather commas, and we must keep writing and let them go as they have destinies of their own to fulfill. This is a tough pill to swallow for most, but your destiny is far greater than anything or anyone who doesn't fit into your story anymore.

The choice of letting go of people you love and care about, but no longer serve a purpose or add value to your life, is one of the toughest to make. Once passed, you will feel as though a weight has been lifted off your shoulders and you will be propelled further into your life mission. Again, love and destiny go hand in hand. They always dance gracefully together, interchanging roles, never stepping on the other's toes. Love fuels destiny and vice versa. You cannot and will not have one without the other. Always remember that....

Love & Destiny

Love and destiny
go hand in hand,
never missing the
chance to dance.

Interchanging
leading roles.
Never stepping
on the other's toes.

Love will never
keep you away
from your destiny,
your destiny will
never keep you
away from love.

Willow Tree

You are far
more stronger
than any test
you will ever face,
and every challenge
comes with it,
preparation for
a better day.

The storms in life,
they come but
they never stay,
like willow trees
in the wind,
you bend,
but never
break.

Insight

—◊—

The willow tree is one of the toughest, more flexible, and enduring trees on the face of the earth. It is one of the few trees that can withstand the strongest conditions of winds, bending almost effortlessly without breaking. For many ages, the willow tree has been metaphorically referenced for those traveling along a spiritual path and amongst symbolic references for life situations in general.

The willow tree reminds us to yield and surrender to the process of life, allowing the winds of change to carry away the things that no longer serve a higher purpose in our lives, as they swiftly replace them with things that do. We must indeed let go of old things so that new things may come and grow. Thus, for those who are entering or traveling on the path of spirituality, this is of great importance. The spiritual path calls for change; change in what we eat, think, and change in our overall lifestyle.

When faced with these changes, the willow asks us to bend with Mother Nature as she lovingly introduces us to many spiritual challenges that prompt us to develop our patience and our ability to endure.

Endurance and patience are some of the greatest spiritual gifts that one can develop. There may be occasions when the storms of confusion run rampant in your mind and you are tempted to go back to your old ways of thinking and living, but don't let this discourage you.

As a person steps into the spiritual path they are literally challenging the consciousness of this realm and its very nature. The chains of material nature are very strong and do not take well to those great souls who try to break free from its clutches. As you do so, it's imperative that you ask the divine for the strength to endure and the patience to learn the lesson at hand. Breaking away from old ways of thinking and living is no easy task for anyone, but it must be done if one is serious about seeking what the soul is trying to find.

The willow tree is also remarkable in the fact that its branches, if they were to fall off, can be planted and used to grow new trees. For us, this symbolically represents our ability to create new opportunities even when we are met with losses. It is also symbolic of how, when broken, we can still be used for a far greater purpose.

God often uses the flawed, imperfect, and broken to spread the messages of His grace and goodness in this world. In the stories of the Bible this is also found to be true. Noah was a drunk, Jacob was a liar, Isaac was a day dreamer, and Elijah was suicidal. The list of imperfect men and women God used is endless and we too can be used by Him in our own special way.

There is not one test in life that you will face that you are not strong enough to overcome. Willow provides us with the inspiration to overcome all that we are faced with. She holds, within her the spirit, the courage, perseverance, and ability to adapt to current conditions.

As we face challenges and fear arises, she reminds us to completely let go and be open to understand and express our innermost emotions and thoughts. When thoughts and emotions are suppressed, they become the catalyst for unwanted stress and eventually cause us to doubt ourselves and our beliefs.

The moon-driven and water-seeking willow tree encourages us to express ourselves emotionally, thus allowing us to heal our spirit and face the path ahead without fear or doubt.

When up against the storms in life, have the attitude of gratitude, give thanks for the test at hand, for it is only in test that we progress. The Lord will never place anything on you that you cannot bare to hold and, with His grace, you will succeed in overcoming.

Be like the willow tree: tough, enduring, and flexible. Let the energy of fearlessness, love, and bliss fill your spirit. You are Divine.

Seeds Of Success

Never be afraid of
achieving your best,
I've heard that a bird
cannot fly without
leaving its nest,
and every failure
comes with it a
seed of success,
as long as you
have God on your
side there is no
reason to stress.

A Tree For Your Dreams

If you planted a tree
for every dream that
you had in your soul,
a beautiful forest
would grow in
the valleys below.

All of the highs in life
help balance the lows,
as long as you grow,
that's what matters
the most.

Tranquility

I just want to live a life
of prosperity and growth.
Though I'm not into taking
pictures, my greatest wish
is to take a selfie of my soul.

I leave my phone at home
because I realize the greatest
moments are captured with
my memory.

Not to be shared with the world
because I see the value in
tranquility.

Insight

—m—

With the advent of social media and reality TV, more time and attention than necessary is being invested in the lives of celebrities, friends, and strangers. We have millions of photos and videos at our fingertips.

Social media has given us the ability to share every moment we experience with the world and we have taken full advantage of this. It's almost as if there's a certain intimacy with life and nature that has been lost because we have substituted our memories of the experience with pictures in our camera rolls.

Nature brings us peace and allows us to connect with our inner nature. However, we limit this experience when we rely on technology to be our eyes, ears, and mind.

Some of the greatest moments you'll ever experience are alone or with those whom you may be with. These moments, being kept within the confines of your own mind and heart, will give you greater clarity and fulfillment when reminiscing on them at later times.

So many of our memories come from pictures of events that we don't actually remember, and this may be due to the fact that we whip out our camera phones almost mindlessly to capture the moment that we actually miss out on what is happening in real time right in front of us.

Although I too sometimes have the tendency to take pictures when experiencing new places, I have to remind myself that experiencing the moment is much more fulfilling than capturing it. Though they are needed in our lives for personal reasons, I think we all could use a break from our phones and technology to experience natural tranquility.

I encourage you to set aside days or times during your day to be free from technology; take a walk outside, or go on a road trip while doing so. You'd be surprised at how tranquil and less chaotic things are once you begin to live in the "now", embracing wherever you are consciously without using your phone or favorite apps.

The greatest moments of your life will be captured with your memory. Try not to rely on technology to take this away from you. Experience life as it is happening now. Your inner most being deserves it.

Indigenous

I sit back and reminisce,
thinking about the future
of my past life, am I really
living or just making
earthly appearances.

To be an inspiration to those
who suffer while serving
these life sentences,
until I return home,
wherever she may be,
indigenous.

Insight

—◊—

There is a certain something embedded within the very fabric of our souls that lets us know that we come from someplace, that we are going someplace, and that one day we will return to that place from which we originated.

While we are here, bound by time and space, let us serve and inspire mankind to further its evolution until destiny calls us home.

Bliss

We dream of a place
that's far more peaceful
than this reality.
Transcending our
physical anatomy,
into a place where there
is no time or space,
just love between galaxies.
Living life naturally,
instead of paycheck
to paycheck,
balancing salaries.

I know a place.

Satcitānanda

Sometimes we wish we could just
look at our lives through a telescope,
and maybe see what's ahead
because today just feels
like another bad episode.
It's like we've planted our seeds
and watered them with our tears,
but it seems like they never grow,
but the universe loves you
more than you would ever know

I bet you never knew
galaxies existed in you,
and you had the power to manifest
anything that you wished to be true.
Just find a way to love yourself
and your enemies too,
and at this moment you'll
find a God that has always
existed in you.

Recognizing your spiritual
divinity is much like the trinity,
though we are not the creator
we are from the same energy,
if we learned to love
we could live until infinity.
If we learned to love
we would live to INFINITY.

What do you know
about living forever,
in a place where time
doesn't exist but we still
spend it together.

What do you know
about living for better,
in peace, love, and happiness
on so many unlimited levels.

Insight

—◦◦◦—

Reflecting on my life up until this point I'm not sure how I made it this far. Although I've been blessed with a certain level of talent, wisdom, and a gift to reach people through words, I've dealt with severe depression and thoughts that are sometimes detrimental and suicidal. I've also been hypersensitive all of my life, something that causes me to feel and experience every emotion seemingly to the "10th Power."

For the most part, life has been an emotional roller coaster. Sometimes I ask, why me? Is life really supposed to be this hard? Why is it when one door opens, another one is slammed in my face?

Being extremely empathetic, there are often times I find myself almost in tears because this world seems so harsh and cruel and I would like to do so much more not only for myself, but for the world around me.

In the past, my love for giving and helping the world sometimes seemed useless. It's as if at times I was a prisoner of my own mind and thoughts to the point where I didn't feel like living. Up until recently, I've always felt this way, but I know I've been given this voice, this struggle, and these gifts to help make this human experience better for all of us.

Therefore, I made a promise to myself, after a near self-inflicted death experience, to always speak the truth and to be completely transparent. No matter how much I gain or don't, how many social media followers I have at any particular time, or how much I have materially, I have never missed the opportunity to let you know that you are not alone.

Although it has taken me many years and downfalls, I've overcome the stages of deep depression and I attribute this to the simple fact that I began to self-love. I stopped letting people and things determine my emotions. I started spending more time alone, doing things that I loved to do, and being comfortable in my own energy. It's like a whole new world opened up to me and I was able to calm those "inner voices."

Self-love brought me that reciprocated energy that I longed for in a relationship. It showed me how to appreciate myself and be content with what I was becoming. It was when I began to self-love that I became aware of my spiritual self and found God.

The title of this particular poem "sat-cit-ānanda" refers to the quality or attributes of God; eternal, full of knowledge, and bliss. *Sat* means eternal, *cit* means knowledge, and *ānanda* means bliss.

As human beings, we all come from the same source, God, and we also possess these qualities but on a much smaller scale. It is my belief that if we simply learn to love ourselves first, and then each other, we can unlock the doors to eternal life, knowledge, and bliss.

By practicing self-love we can learn to accept others for who they are, because in their flaws, we can see the things we have once overcome or may be currently dealing with. In addition, self-love will allow you to receive levels of divine enlightenment from God. Self-love will bring you the eternal peace and happiness you've been yearning for.

To not love yourself would be to deny your spiritual existence. I speak from experience when I say that "self-love saved my life".

Original Self

We spend our entire lives looking for
soul-mates but never come to the
full realization of the soul inside.
Being blinded by misconceptions
like complexion with the perception
that we have three open eyes.

I've traveled through many galaxies
with this spiritual knowledge,
just to let you know that you
are not these physical bodies.

I'm not too naive to believe
my perception is right,
but I think it's time we
stopped investing in vice,
and get back to our
spiritual conception of life.

Maybe we started feeling ourselves
because we're living in wealth,
But there is still so much
pain and suffering
because we have lost touch
with our original self.

Insight

—⚭—

With the exception of religious purpose, the average person rarely questions their existence in this world. The questions of "Why am I here?", "What is the purpose of all life?" or "Why I am suffering?" may never arise.

Some may find it just not worth the research and continue in their search for love, success, money, or other worldly endeavors. The vast majority of people in today's society seem to have no real spiritual concept of life and think more on a physical basis, being caught up in trying to improve and master the physical aspects of this material world. It is my belief that this is due to the lack of proper teaching or guidance and, as a result, we have lost touch with our original spiritual self.

Knowledge is the beginning of our spiritual life and "I am not this body" is the beginning of real truth. You do not have a soul; you are spirit-soul and have a body. The soul is described as atomic in size and is located within the hearts of all living entities. The soul is indestructible, eternal. It is never born and never dies. It's what gives the body life and consciousness to the brain. The fighting amongst nations and race is due to the bodily conception of life. We are saying I am American, I am Iraqi, I am Chinese, and I must protect my home country. There is so much fighting going on over this land. The land has become worshiped, so much that people are willing to sacrifice their lives for it. Why is the land so important to us? It's because the body has grown from it and has a connection to it.

Our attachment to the material is what puts us in so much stress; we are attached to and rely on the physical temporary things for happiness. We are suffering due to the fact that our whole existence is for material enjoyment when instead, it should be for spiritual realization. I see our bodies much like one may see clothing. As one may *have* a shirt, a pair of jeans, or a hat, the person is not these items.

Similarly, though we have these African bodies, American bodies, or Indian bodies we are not to consider ourselves these things. We are in possession of them. Once we begin to look beyond these physical perceptions and designations, getting back to our original state, we will see just how special we are.

The moment we do this, we will be full of joy and excitement as we simply take the time to notice how we are all part of a larger network of energy, all working together to balance each other and manifest God's will for humanity.

Stardust

It's important to realize
karma exists eternally
based on everything
that you do first.

Caterpillars evolve
into butterflies,
to exemplify
that which you call
death is only a new birth.

The purpose of life is not
to accumulate more wealth,
but to identify and
liberate your soul-self.

Spiritual Sky

I think it's very clear
that we're only here
for a limited time,
every day we see
people living and dying,
but we've yet to invest
in our spiritual side.

I just want us all to
transcend this world
of criminal minds,
and subliminal lies,
and spend eternity in
a spiritual sky.

Insight

—◊◊◊—

All that we see and experience in this physical world is a temporary manifestation of material nature. Aside from the individual soul, everything is under the regulation of natural laws of matter, and passes through six stages of existence.

The first of the six stages is birth, then the object or person grows, produces some by-products, stays for some time, deteriorates, and then finally dies.

Nothing in contact with material nature can be beyond the previously mentioned laws of existence and, therefore, no one or nothing can be eternally sustained in this world. Granted all men have their vices, but even as we see people go through these stages of life, we still continue to invest in our own demise.

There are things that we know are harmful, or that may even be killing us, that we still continue to indulge in out of illusion and ignorance. These things may include unhealthy food, drinking, smoking, or other things that are harmful to our mind, body, and spirit.

In the back of our minds, we know these things are terribly wrong. However, illusion and addiction effectively entice us to indulge in them. Even with death staring us in the face every moment of every day, those of us who are deeply covered in illusion fail to align themselves spiritually and prepare for life beyond this physical realm.

Just as yesterday we prepared for today, and today we shall prepare for tomorrow, this life is merely preparation for the next and what we do in this hour of our lives determines our placement in the life here after.

The concepts and beliefs of an afterlife are not a new age phenomenon, but have existed throughout the ages and noted by some of the world's most popular religions. Those of Christian faith allude to life hereafter residing in either heaven or hell, while those who are Muslim speak of "the garden" which is to be considered the heavenly paradise of God.

The universe is not only infinite, but there are also an infinite number of universes in existence that contain both hell and heavenly abodes. In our current incarnations, we are not only preparing ourselves for a particular planetary system to live on but also for a particular body we may have in the future. A man or woman who lives in ignorance much like an animal will someday come to take the body of an animal, while a man or woman who lives a more godly life will take birth either as a human or in the abode of gods. This human life is a gift. It is the perfect opportunity for the soul to be liberated to higher planetary systems and, for some, a chance to escape the miseries of birth and death.

It is not my intent to force any specific belief system on you, but it is with great intent to make you aware of these truths and awaken your true spiritual nature. In our current age, all spirituality and religion has been somewhat lost, as we have surrendered to dealings of the lower self, succumbing to temptation, anger, lust, and material desires. The absence of spiritual consciousness has driven us away from our true nature of peace, love, and bliss, into the abyss of material illusion.

Though we are composed of mind, body, and spirit, we must learn to balance them in perfect harmony. If we fail to do so, we further entangle ourselves in this material world and be driven further away from "Home."

Meditation

What if I told you meditation
was better than medication,
and with one breath you could
heal your situation or even
travel to better places.

Transcending this physical
world of separation,
reuniting with our ancestors
on stars and constellations,
practicing levitation.

Though this life is nice
we should live it in preparation,
for the next one, so I'm writing
these revelations.
So when I become an
ancestor my reincarnation
can find peace in this
world of devastation.

Hare Krishna Hare Rama,
no matter or religion
you have to pay homage,
and always speak from
a level of oneness.

Nirvana

It seems this physical
world would rather you
celebrate your goals,
with the focus being on
material gain just to
devastate your foes.

I'm just trying to spread
love every place I go,
when I meditate I grow,
searching for better ways
to elevate my soul.

Matter

What if all of your
dreams and things
became reality?
Would you change,
or maybe rearrange
all the things you
were imagining?

Would you promote
peace and love in
the same manner you
do world tragedies?

Do you think human lives
matter in other galaxies?

What if life made you
choose between frames
of happiness and agony?
What type of pictures
would you hang in your
hearts gallery?

Do you think human lives
matter in other galaxies?

Growing Pains

I know you're
going through
some things and it's
hard to think logical,
and even harder
to be positive
when only failure
seems probable,
but if you trust in God
anything is possible.

You just have to
be willing to grow
through what you
go through,

And to be a
better person,
you have to
be willing to
let go of the
old you.

Second Chance

Sometimes we lose
people we love and
we wonder why
God would take
their time away.

But never let death
define your faith,
nothing really dies,
there is a soul inside
that is given wings
to fly to a higher place.

Maybe they're in heaven
to laugh and dance,
maybe they've been given
a second chance.

Insight

—⧟—

T he average person looks at death with sadness, fear, and resentment, but those who know its nature, realize it to be a beautiful and liberating experience. Our true self, the soul, is eternal and so, in truth, there is no death.

When the soul leaves the body it is much like changing clothes; we leave behind our old bodies and go on to accept new garments according to our deeds and nature in the life that has passed.

Becoming free from the pain and suffering of this world and entering into a place of peace and tranquility, we feel a joy that cannot be experienced in our physical bodies. There is no misery here; no wars, no famine, and none of the stress that is caused by material life. To those who may be suffering due to illness, death is an exit strategy of the soul, because the body that it has is no longer suitable for its power and vastness.

When we look at death objectively and think that we will one day have to give up this body, we sometimes think how God's plan can be cruel and can't imagine Her being the compassionate and merciful mother that She is.

However, when we look at death with the eyes of wisdom, we realize that it is only through the process of death that we exit this world and enter into the astral and spirit world to experience a freedom that is not possible on earth. Death has one purpose and that is to remind you that you cannot die!

As we remember those who have passed on to new worlds or re-entered this one, let us rejoice for they have been given a fresh start and a new beginning. Of course, we would not be human if we didn't miss our loved ones. However, through sincere prayer, we can connect with their being and feel their spirit here on earth.

To send your thoughts to your love ones, sit in silence and meditate upon the name of God. When you feel His presence within you, concentrate your mind on your heart and, as you do so, vocalize your prayers, words, and feelings to the ones that you have lost. Send to that soul your vibrations of love and, as you continue to do so, they will receive your vibrations and transfer comfort and love back to you. They have not forgotten you just like you haven't forgotten them. Practice this technique any time you feel lonely or have the urge to connect with those you have lost on this earthly plane of existence. If you mentally send them your thoughts of love continuously, you are sure to meet with them again.

Know that this current life is not an end, but only a bridge that must be crossed to reunite with God and those we love. Let joy fill your spirit as you remember those you love. They are with you in this moment.

Free Spirit

I see myself in everything,
the stars, moon, planets and trees.
All of life is but a creation
emanating within me.

As I progress on the path of
self-realization I time travel too,
recreating myself in galaxies anew.

The spiritual spark of my soul
provides light in dark times,
in search of nothing at all,
but everything I come to find.

Completely desireless I
surrender to the Divine.

I belong to the universe,
and nothing is mine.

Free from duality and
material bondage,
I give all I have to God
and live abundance.

Goldmines in my mind
and a platinum plated heart,
I allow all things to come
and go as letting go is an art.

My words are paintbrushes
for an empty canvas,
depicting pictures of an age
that has long vanished.

Maybe in time we will
realize the gift of life,
seeing ourselves in
everything as infinite light.

Birds

I wonder if birds try
to fly into outer space,
I want to be that one
that tried and got away.
So many light years
ahead of me, but still,
I fly a mile a day,
enjoying everything
there is to see with
a smiling face.

I never knew this
much existed outside
of my nest and tree,
and searching for things
with grief, but now I
feel extra free.

With peace and ecstasy I
travel through shadows of light,
comets and meteorites remind
me of my perilous flight.
As my wings seem to carry
me with passionate strikes,
My soul seeks to find what
truly matters in life.

Am I meant to live like
an animal or think beyond
this physical nature?
While most of my population
is satisfied with living in cages,
I've always dreamed of
intergalactic travel and
spiritual places.

Amazingly crazy how my
thoughts have manifested to be,
resting and reminiscing on a star
I think of those that I left in the tree.

I hope that other birds are
inspired to fly into outer space.
Maybe one day they'll try
and fly away.

Astral Light

What if I told you that
this was nothing more
than a distant dream,
that only existed in the
mind of God, everyday
is just a different scene.

You and I little beams,
casted upon the shadows
of a bigger screen.
In the beginning it was
the Word which gave
life to living things.

Different beings spring
from that one True Light,
He came unto his own,
but not many knew Christ.
But as many as received Him,
to them , He gave a new life,
and the power to become Sons
of God, witnesses of that blue light.

Beneath this physical
body is an astral light,
that which you shall
return to after this life.
Death is but an illusion
the passing of night,
All men shall reach God
with the passion of Christ,
And return to that astral light,
After this life.

Pray To

People may hate you
because of who you pray to
but never mind that, you
have faith and stay true,
everything will be okay too.

Maybe sometimes you want
to cry and that's okay too,
just remember every breakdown
is preparing you for your break through.
All that matters is that you pray
and God is who you pray to.

Insight

—ᴠᴠ—

The main purpose of human life is to inquire about the absolute truth and develop one's consciousness from material knowledge to the platform of spiritual knowledge and God consciousness. Amongst the masses of new age spiritualists and what is deemed to be the "conscious community," there are a few rare souls who fully comprehend and accept this.

Actually, real consciousness is God consciousness or knowledge in the absolute, and all other levels of consciousness are temporary. The source of all creation known as the Absolute, or God, is eternal, full of knowledge, and bliss, thus consciousness centered in Him is of this nature.

He is the omnipresent, all pervading super-soul within all living entities in this material world. The material world is but a temporary manifestation of God's creation and, due to the laws of nature, it is subject to changes that prohibit it from enduring the ultimate test of time. All that exists in this world is temporary and subject to illusion and thus any level of consciousness centered in worldly matters are of this nature. When one transcends all other levels of consciousness and enters into God consciousness, he slowly lifts this veil of illusion and progressively attains to knowledge that is eternal.

There are many pseudo-spiritualists, atheists, and individuals who deem themselves to be conscious, but deny God's existence and debate the validity of His incarnations. For those of us who live, work, and socialize with these individuals who make such claims, it can be troubling at times to be content in our faith and religious practices.

The denial of God is not a 21st century trend. Rather, many people have denied it for many ages. Actually, it is because of our wanting to forget God that we are granted this human form, thus it is expected that there will be a denial of His existence.

When the spirit soul seeks to venture off into the vast existence of God's creation, God, being the loving and compassionate father that He is, gives us an opportunity to take birth in this human form. When taking birth in the human form, we subject ourselves to temporariness, illusion, forgetfulness of our natural god state, and forgetfulness of our Creator. It is only after many, many births that one accepts this truth. Seeking to end the miseries that come with this human life, a person then makes the inquiry about why they are suffering, the nature of their self-soul, the Creator, and then in the process, finally awakens within themselves their spiritual consciousness.

From personal experience, once being one conscious individuals, I can say that it was only inquiry and the awakening of a new level of cons⌐ ⌐⌐⌐⌐ss that I realized how much illusion I was under.

Everything that I speak in poetic form and in summary, is a result of entering into this God consciousness. The things that I almost effortlessly express without prior knowledge or studying, are proof alone of the power of this level of consciousness. God consciousness reigns supreme because it is our natural state of consciousness and, when we seek and revert back to our natural state, by the grace of God, all things are reviled unto us to know and understand.

Contrary to popular belief, believing in and serving God does not make you a "sheep." Again, the main purpose of life is to acquire God consciousness, liberate ourselves from this material world, and re-enter the kingdom of Heaven. Many people discredit the savior Jesus Christ or many other incarnations of God, because of the evil things that have been done in the name of religion.

Man has tarnished and misrepresented religion so much that individuals who are seeking to understand higher are afraid to do so out of fear of being labeled a "sheep" among many other things.

Over the ages and till this day, man, due to his greed, has killed, enslaved, taken land, and started wars, all in the name of religion. It is for this reason that God incarnates himself, sends His son, or devotee to this earthly realm, with the purpose of reclaiming His children and re-teaching the principles of religion to lost souls.

The main goal of all religion is to help one to develop God consciousness so that we may be fit to enter into spiritual realms and live amongst God. Although God has no religion, it has been manifested by man due to the truths and teachings that God incarnations have left on earth before their departure.

When we accept religion with this understanding, we fully realize its purpose and the benefits of our religious practices. Real religion is dharma and that is surrender, accompanied by devotional service to God and this is how we are granted access into the spirit world.

God can only be realized fully or known through the process of devotional service and, thus, the atheistic cannot know Him because they are not willing to build a relationship with Him.

Regardless of what others may say of your God, you are encouraged to have unwavering faith in your spiritual journey. You cannot expect others who don't have a relationship with God, or even attempt to have one, to understand your connection to and belief in Him.

This type of dry speculation about the absolute is "frog's philosophy." There was once a frog that lived in a well. One day, a bird landed in the well and told many stories about the Atlantic Ocean; its beauty, and vastness. The frog could not believe it. He had seen birds and other animals who came to the well, but never heard of the things the bird was describing. The bird told him about fish and giant sea animals, amongst other things, but the frog wouldn't accept his commentary. After hours of questioning and debating, the frog still was not able to accept what the bird was telling him. Realizing that his attempts were futile, the bird made his peace with the frog and headed back to enjoy the sights and sounds of the ocean. In short, the frog's philosophy about the ocean was relative. Because he lived in the well his entire life, he was not able to grasp the concept of its vastness and the creatures that lived in the ocean. In this same way, those who pass false judgments on you because of your beliefs, are doing so from a relative point of view. Until these individuals see, feel, and choose to understand the vastness of God, they will never come to know His greatness and glory.

We all have different faiths, but there is only one Eternal truth and this truth is God. His incarnations are like different instruments playing the same song–the song of surrender and service. As you pray, seek to know God more and develop your relationship. Surrender to His will in your life, and choose to serve Him in all that you do.

I can say that a life lived in God consciousness is the greatest feeling ever. It's always blissful and the sun is always shining. Those who lose their lives in God are remembered eternally.

Spiritual Beings

As we look into
the night sky,
mesmerized by
the moon and
little lights,
it is She who
illuminates every
thing and the Power
that has given life.

For those who truly
seek to know God,
see that woman is
the risen Christ.,
She is the Kundalini
that fills the spirit
when its rivers dry.

It may take you many
lives to accept this
message that has been
given unto me from
dimension five.
Know that God is always
with you not only
when you die, but as
you are still alive

She is two sides of
the moon, Gemini,
both masculine
and feminized.
It is her love
that heals when
water falls and
rivers cry.

It may be many nights
that you weep over
material things,
crying yourself to sleep
while loving a dream.
Know that these
things are seasonal
like winter and spring.
Free yourself from these
dreams and become
spiritual beings.

Give your life to God
and be given your wings.
Become spiritual beings.

Love & Relationships

Love Is.

Love is that emotional,
spiritual thing inside
that you can't define.

From afar it looks
like a danger sign,
but as you get closer
it's almost like you're
looking into an angel's eyes,
because they make you
forget about everything
that has ever hurt you
and the pain inside.

And smile as bright as
the sunshine, even though
it may rain at times.

Sacred

Love is scared and
love is sanctified.
It is what brought
peace to the world
in ancient times.

Love is the same
energy that created
the universe and
paints the sky.

Love is the reason
that birds sing at night
and angels fly

Mind

Love is intellectual
conversations that
make our brains collide.

.....

Love can really make
you go insane at times.

Feelings

Love is that little thing inside
that makes anger die.

Self

Love told me
to love myself,
and then I
became sublime.

Unexplainable

Love really can't be
explained at times.
Love is everything
that I can't describe.

Everything

Love is everything.
Everything is Love.

Sunrise

Have you ever
seen the sunrise
in one's eyes,
it is beauty
that makes the
moon jealous
when the sun dies,
and your mouth
and mind get
tongue tied,
trying to express
the feelings within
your confines.

And all of these things
combine sometimes
to make the things
inside unwind.

You give meaning
to the sunrise,
and the reason
that the sun shines.

My sunrise.

Flowers

Way before you grew
I knew you'd be the
most beautiful flower
this world has ever seen,
my only wish and deed
is to water your seeds,
until you grow larger
than anyone could
ever dream.

Always encouraging you
to love yourself and
increase your self-esteem,
although I believe all the
butterflies and bees in
paradise have yet to rest
their wings on better things.

Yes, indeed you are more
than just a sight to see,
you are everything that
weeds and trees would
like to be.

Like sunflowers when
the sun rises you bring
life to me.

My Goddess

It is with you that
I choose to share
my sublime feelings.
You are what the
universe is made of,
beautiful, divine,
women.

Though your skin is
like silk compared
to fine linen, it is the
ocean of your soul
that defies limits.
Maybe you should
find the time to
love yourself
and dive in it.

You are the beauty
and the essence of life,
and the main reason
I count my blessings
at night.

You make angels
blush in your presence,
you are such a precious
delight.

I think I found
heaven tonight.

So many stars in the sky, oh my,
but you are the brightest one,
you possess enough power
in your smile to light the sun.

You are divine, the righteous one,
I found you and I stopped waiting
for Christ to come.

My Goddess.

Sunset

From my perception
it seems like everything
in life is too redundant,
but I want to know
everything about you
except what you
do for money.

Living in a generation
that bases its relations
on compensation.

I want to look into your
eyes and see constellations,
there's nothing better than
sunsets and deep conversations.

Breathing you

You are the only star
that would shine as
the night recedes.
I thought love had died
but you resurrected it
like Christ in me.

You give me life to breath,
you are like the trees,
so nice and sweet,
you make life complete.

Soul Food

I really don't
think heaven has
seen a prettier face,
you are indeed
more precious
than diamonds
that sit in a safe.
Even if angels
had your heart in
captivity I would
take a chance to
steal it away.

Of course I love God,
but I praise you in
a much similar way.

You are soul food
to me without
fixing a plate.

Sometimes I thank
God for you,
before I finish
my grace.

Summer Daze

I'm dreaming of
a summer day.
With palm trees
and sunny rays,
in sunflower fields
we run away.
We run away.
We run way.

We run away.

Peach

There is nothing more
pleasing than seeing
the sweetness in a
woman's eyes.
It is like tasting the
sweetness of peaches
in the summer time.

It even makes flowers
in fall come alive,
and the harshness of
winter embrace
its sunny side.

Sweet as a peach
in the summer time,
you give me a reason
to come alive.

Sweet as a peach
in the summer time.
If only we could see
the world through a
woman's eyes.

Divine Feminine

To know God,
study woman.
She is the creator.
The intelligence.
Eternally loving,
eternally forgiving.

She is what brings
peace and balance.
She is the giver
of all forms of life.

She is the beauty
in all things.

It is feminine energy
which holds the entire
cosmos within a spec
of her shimmering eyes.

It is She who is God.

Simplicity

Your black is
such a beautiful
masterpiece.

Deeply decoded
within the moon
and the stars,
I search for
your heart in
every galaxy.

Post Armageddon

Can we have 2 AM
conversations under
the star lights?
Leaving all of our problems
and negativity at home
and know that everything
will be alright,
As long as we have
each other in our lives.

Can we not label
anything as ridiculous
and just let our
thoughts be endless?
Can we manifest this
moment in infinence?

Astral Love

I will never let
the windows to
my soul lie to you.
I see so much
potential in us. I also
see a universe
inside of you.

Even in my deepest
meditations I couldn't
imagine these things.

Until I met you on
the astral plane.
That is when
happiness came.

Promises

I've been broken
many times and
I promise it's a
mess trying to put
these pieces together.

So before we make
any more promises,
promise me you
believe in forever.

If I died protecting you,
I promise you I'll save
your seat in heaven,
just so in the next
lifetime we can
be together.

I promise

Reflections

I'm sorry they
made you hate
your reflection.

So much so that
you hide it behind
make up and a
little mascara,
just to feel like
you'll make more
progression.

In a world that's so
stuck up on physical
enhancements.

And the media trying
to redesign you,
but never let what's
behind you, define you.
Real beauty is inside you.

Melanin Queen

I know we live
In a society that
makes you feel
like your looks
mean everything.

Intelligence seems,
somewhat over-looked,
because guys feel like
they can give you the
world by selling
you dreams.

But they really don't
know these are
irrelevant things,
because you already
had the universe in
your possession.

Melanin Queen.

Beautiful Black Woman

I find it so amazing
that you still exhibit
love even though you've
been hurt too many times.

Beautiful black woman,
Is see the stars in your
complexion and the
moon in your eyes.

African Gem

You are more
like an angel in
a human disguise,
as soon as I make
it back to heaven,
the first thing I'll
do is paint pictures
of you in the sky.

You have such
a beautiful mind,
and immaculate
natural skin.

All the diamonds
in the world do not
compare to you.

My African Gem

Black Girl Soul

I love everything about you,
your blackness is greatness.

With the soul of a million suns,
you inspire the happiest face

Black Girl Tone

Beautiful soul,
magical skin.

Her Smile

For I do not know
the darkness that
is to be displayed
in this life to come.

But it is woman who
possesses enough
power in her smile
to light the sun.

We may say that
heaven is some
place inside of space.

But in woman
there is enough
power to ignite
the brightest day.

Balance

I realize sometimes
we're going to be
mad at each other
and have attitudes,
but that doesn't
equate to the
pain I would
feel without me
having you.

Our feelings won't
always be compatible,
so I give you latitude,
but I still show you the
utmost gratitude.
Thank you for letting
me balance you.

I never really knew
what love could be.
Well that's up until the point
I knew you fell in love with me.
I know at times we both feel
like we should get up and leave,
I thank you for never
giving up on me.

In You

As I look into
your eyes I see
constellations.

There is nothing
better than sunsets
and deep conversations.

Eros Logos

I've realized love has
no perfect reflection
and can never be fully
reciprocated because
it's all based on the other
person's perception,
of love, but that doesn't
mean we can't have
the perfect connection.

All it takes is the
mentality to do right.
What is the sunshine
without the balances
of the moonlight?

Biology

I believe love is less about
possession and more
about appreciation,
even through trials
and tribulations,
we stay committed
with no deviations.

Just because you're
beautiful I'm not to treat
you like a commodity,
because it's less about
your anatomy,
and more about your
biology**.**

A Million

Maybe you're that rose
that grew from concrete
and humble beginnings.

Never realizing your
worth because you had
to funnel feelings,
into a person or
a relationship that
always seemed to
come with limits.

But even if a man
were to encounter
hundreds of women,
he should always
see you as one
in a million.

Where Love Overflows

She has as endured so much in love,
yet and still remains so optimistic
in her journey towards discovering
someone who actually appreciates
everything she has grown to be.

And even still in this journey she
encounters those who may be less
deserving of the kind of love she
has to offer, she proceeds for the
sake of experiencing love even though
there's a sort of imbalance in effort
and emotional connection. It's sort of like
she's pouring a gallon container of water into a
12-oz bottle, her love seems to overflow.

Having so much love to give, she has yet to
encounter an individual who is able to be a vessel
to receive all of the love that she pours into them.

This may cause her to question her worth
because she's doing all that she can to make
things work but it seems like it's never enough.
Or maybe it's too much?

A bit confused, she begins to dim her light,
reducing herself to a simple spark to try to
accommodate to her male counterparts "glow".

It's quite uncomfortable for her and as
time proceeds she returns back to her true nature.
She comes to understand she is not the problem,
though she may have made some poor choices
in men she forgives herself and grows from
the experience like she always does.

There are as many women to choose
from as there are stars in the sky
but she knows she is the one.

In a million.

She kept shinning.

This is you

Seeds

We have to stop
treating our women
like commodities,
show more respect,
and be more encouraging
of her modesty

Because the true essence
and the presence of a
woman is never obsolete.
Speak life into her soul
give her more to see,
because beautiful flowers
never grow without
watering seeds.

Rain Drops

Maybe we should
try growing in love
instead of falling in it,
because every time we land
our feelings advance,
but in the wrong direction
it's like they all diminish.

It's a blessing to
have someone who
sticks beside you even
when the rain drops,
someone who's there
for you unconditionally,
helping, making
sure the pain stops.

The Healer

Why do you try
to force yourself
into situations that
you don't need to,
failing to realize
that before you
pour yourself into
someone they must
first be a vessel to
hold and receive you.

Don't let your deceitful
ego mislead you,
the more you try
to pour yourself
into a broken vessel
it will overflow and
leak through.

And that's what
seems to defeat you,
because you try to
be the healer in
ill situations that
you're not meant
to treat through.

See through the blind
illusions of your own
mind games.
You have to
understand
that people and
times change,
and you can't
walk back into
the same hurtful
doors expecting
not to find pain.

Letting go is easy,
but we make it
seem challenging,
because we are
so caught up in
the memories,
and not focused
on the reality.

Insight

——❦——

Y ou are what is referred to in this piece as "the healer." This is one of your natural gifts and the reason why you are so loved amongst those you have close relationships with. You are the one person others can count on when dealing with personal issues and are in need of someone they can talk to, as you are very understanding and can assist them in their troubles without passing any judgment upon them. You can be counted on to give moral support, level headed advice, or sometimes simply an ear for others to vent to.

As the healer, you have remarkable patience and a strong tolerance when it comes to dealing with negativity. Compassionate, kind, and warm by nature, you have a keen interest in pleasing and serving others. Your life revolves around helping people, sometimes even at the risk of getting hurt yourself. You are the healer and, as gifted as you are at doing so, this is also at times one of your greatest faults.

When in a relationship, you are willing to sacrifice your emotions and needs for the well-being and happiness of your partner. You feel as though it is your duty to help them out of any emotional, financial, or mental rut that they may have found themselves in. Of course, you are expected to assist them in these matters, but you over-extend yourself, even when previous attempts to help solve their problems have proven to be futile, you stand strong in your nature.

Exhausting your gift as the healer, you then become an enabler, allowing them to dump all of their emotional baggage on you and not giving them a chance to grow from their own pain. As the healer, you have yet to understand that it's okay to take a hand off your magic wand and allow your partner to overcome their own storms, as this is the only way they will truly learn and grow.

Another issue you have with being the healer is not knowing when it's time to let go of toxic and hurtful situations and begin to heal yourself. Being obsessed with your nature, you sometimes find it hard to realize that there are some people who can't be healed, at least by you. Forcing yourself to heal a broken situation can really drain you and you have to know that the more you try to do so, the more you will leave yourself open to being hurt as well.

A person can become so broken that they begin to break and hurt everyone they come in contact with. At times, the pride of being "the healer" will stop you from seeing this, as you feel sorry for the person and, thinking you can save the day, you try with extreme effort to help them see that situations are not so bad and that they can overcome them.

Although there is hope for everyone to overcome struggles and be healed, it is only possible if they themselves choose to do so.

Only you can heal you; this is a lesson to be learned regardless of the type of relationship, whether it be with friends, life partners, or family. When you allow others to be the source of your healing, you also allow them to be the source of your brokenness.

The healer must heal themselves and encourage others to do so for themselves. You must never overstep this boundary, allowing yourself to be the source of healing and happiness for somebody else. We must all look within ourselves for happiness and allow others only to add to the joy, happiness, and bliss that we have found within us.

Brokenness

Sometimes we
fall in love with
broken things.
Like broken people,
we hope and dream,
to one day heal
their broken wings.

Relationships are
about oneness,
but believing in two,
but even in their
brokenness you
can sometimes
find pieces of you.

Types

Broken people,
break people.

Hurt people,
hurt people

Healed people
heal people.

It is often that
we search and
fall in love
with ourselves.

Situations

Your partner in life
should wish to bring
out the best in you
and not just want to
have sex with you,
but maybe show you
a side of yourself that's
more intellectual,
and be your peace when
this world is stressing you.

Anybody can generate some lies,
just to penetrate your thighs,
but who can liberate your mind.

Body and soul.

Cold Cases

They say love is not
what it used to be.
That's only because
we're not making
ourselves available
to one person
exclusively.

Because truthfully,
we'd rather be "friends"
with quotations,
and end up getting
hurt in that situation,
because it never
goes places.

Cold cases.

Love Lessons

No matter your
situation never
let a break up
defeat you.

I know that
the healing is
a long procedure,
but you have
to stop relying
on people to
complete you.

When you become
a diamond
you'll see why
life had to
pressure you.

Because some
people just come
along for us to
learn a lesson through.

Attraction

Attraction can
be a distraction.
Though the product
may look good,
we don't realize
what we're getting
until we open
the package.

Because some
people come with
emotional baggage,
and ex problems,
in real life,
because they
never took the
time to heal right.

Emergency

Sometimes you
have to start
giving less of you.
Especially if you
feel like you're
constantly being
disrespected and
neglected too.
Maybe distance
will get the
message through.

You should never
expect someone
to love you perfectly,
but they should
always love
you with a
sense of urgency.

Like it's
an emergency.

Last Words

It's not your
fault that you've
never been
treated right,
but once you
find someone
who feels like
everything you
need in life,
make sure you
treat them right.

Because people
have a tendency
to hold on
to past hurt,
never realizing
what they have
until they are
speaking their
last words.

For Love

You become emotionally
damaged when they take
your emotions for granted,
because you're not too
overly demanding,
and just a little bit too
lenient and that's the
inconvenience of being
a hopeless romantic.

Maybe you're just
in love with the idea
so you rush into love.

Maybe you're just a
sucker for love.

Rejection

It's impossible
to be in a situation
that is nothing but bliss,
but being with the wrong
person will have you
feeling like love just
doesn't exist.

It's like pulling teeth
when all you wanted
was a hug and a kiss.

A little affection.

There's nothing worse
than being in love but
feeling rejected.

After-Math

Maybe it's math
that makes
relationships
so difficult.
If it's real then
it's unconditional,
there's no need
for reciprocals.

Love should
be multiplied by
one but never
divided in two.
Even if they
subtracted,
you should always
find absolute
love in you.

Genuine Simplicity

People will take
for granted those
who are easy to please.
It's like they would
rather stick around
to hurt you because you
haven't seen the obvious
reasons to leave.

When you do
they ask for
forgiveness
and sympathy,
because it's always
hard to find someone
with that sort of
genuine simplicity.

Mirrors

Naturally we all
seek and expect
affectionate love.
But everyone that
we encounter
is simply a
reflection of us.

Maybe sent from
divine spirit
to give us direction
and such,
or show us who
we truly are
to influence a new
creation of us.

Lifetime

We live in a time
where people are
so in a rush to be
in a relationship,
to fulfill a void or
perceived vacancy.

Abrasively chasing
situations that
leave us defeated,
not realizing or
believing, you were
already blessed
with all the love
that you ever needed.

In this lifetime.

Excessive Behavior

Take a few things
into consideration
before you
lay together,
even if it's good
it's never going
to be great enough
to make you
stay together,
and once you
start having sex
things can get
confusing on
a major level.

Feelings get
over excessive
needing constant
reassurance
just to know
you're protected.

Last Time

Do you remember
last time,
you said it was
the last time?

And here you are
fifth last time,
It's like you
break each other's
hearts just to pass time.

Maybe it's past time,
that you let go
and let grow,
individually,
or hold on to this
one last time,
until infinity.

For-Never-Ever

Some things last forever,
Some things never.

But blessed are
those who
see the beauty
in both situations,
that made them better.

Forgiveness means
you're ready to fly,
because you've walked
through hell, but was able
to find heaven inside.

Broken Vases

Falling in love
can be a tragedy,
or a beautiful
masterpiece,
if you let it happen
naturally.

All it really takes
is time and patience,
to see what exists
behind smiling faces.

It's better to love at
the slowest pace,
because you never want
to put your pretty flowers
in a broken vase.

Love Enemies

Never confuse energy
with chemistry,
just because the vibe
is right doesn't mean
it's meant to be.

You were thinking
love for infinity.
They were thinking
a few moments
of intimacy.

That relationship
has no symmetry.
And That's how
sex friends become
love enemies.

Used To Be

I'm sorry I'm not
who I used to be.
I guess I used to
be a sucker for love
but I promise there's
no more using me.

I used to love you
like there was two of me,
but I really can't be mad
because I'm glad of
what I grew to be.

I guess that's how it
goes usually.

Eulogy

In order for you to grow
you have to stop watering
dead situations.

Even though deep in
your heart you may
feel sad inside.

That pain is only
temporary there is
no need to agonize.

One day you will be
glad it died.

Light Inside

So what if no one
understands you,
all that matters
is that you learn
to light your
own candles.

In other words
the light inside.
So when times
get dark you can
always see things
on the brighter side,
because you have
that light inside.

Feels

Haven't they told you
that love can be
naive instead of blind,
but regardless of what
you are going through
you have to believe
in better times.

I know you're at a
point that you want
to settle down, so you
pray that things
happen to work,
but sometimes you
have to put your pride aside
and put your happiness first.

Nowhere Fast

You do realize that every
relationship comes with
a price to pay?
What if you stayed
and threw the rest of
your life away?
How many chances have
you given them to
get it right today?

How many tears have
you have had to wipe away
to hide your pain?

Is your destination really
worth your drive insane?

Doves Cry

Nobody really wants to
be alone and it's human
nature to be passionate,
but somebody continues
to hurt you. Why do you
accept them back again?

Are you willing to sacrifice
a few extra months in
exchange for your happiness?

Maybe you're also afraid
of being alone and that's
the only thing stopping you,
but it's never too late
or impossible to find
love in solitude.

I know it may bother you
and inside of you it feels
like when doves cry,
but sometimes it's more
than okay for you to let
go and maybe let love die.

Chances

When someone truly
loves you don't take
them for granted,
because no matter
how deep their
feelings may be,
they may not come
with second chances.

All that is needed
is reassurance
and understanding,
so never miss the
chance to express
your feelings and
be romantic.
Because by any chance,
those chances could vanish.

9 Gates

Relationships are
wonderful but
never compromise
your dignity,
just because you're
lonely and want
someone there
physically to help
ease your misery.

There are plenty
of fine faces,
so many of us
blind dating.

But it's better
to find patience
than to end up
having your
time wasted.

Ex's

There's a big
difference between
I want you and
I need you.

If they really
wanted you
they would have
done the things
they needed to,
to keep you.

Seasons

I know that God
blessed us all with
the vision to see,
other fish in the sea,
but when things get
tough don't think your
puzzle's incomplete,
or missing a piece.

All relationships
have their seasons,
the good, the bad,
and in between it,
so if you find some-
thing worth keeping,
to make excuses
to leave it.

The soul mate is one who
will lead you back to God.

Self-Love

Of all relationships,
the ones we have
with ourselves are
the most important.

We make ourselves
vessels for the love
that we wish to receive,
by first pouring that
love into ourselves.

The Road

On the road to happiness
there is no final destination,
and everyone that hurt you
will fade with time and separation.

Divine Affirmation

When I grow up,
I want to be divine.
I want to be aligned,
with the stars, moon,
galaxies in the sky.

I'm going to love myself
and awaken my soul inside.
I'm going to walk with pride,
head up high.

I'm going to dream so big,
spread my wings and fly.

When I die,
I want to feel alive,
I am eternal,
I am divine.
I am divine.
I am divine.
I AM.
DIVINE.

Divine Soul

I do not waste my
time trying to find gold,
I have all of these
things within me,
I am divine soul.

I possess all of the
beauty of a sunflower
within my glow.

I am eternal sunshine,
I pose, and time froze.
My mind flows,
with thoughts as
deep as the mind goes.
Swim within my abode,
and find gold.

I am not this body
within my clothes,
I am divine soul.

My Black Is A Blessing

Did you not know
your black is a blessing?
When angels fell on earth
they made Africa heaven,
the first to be birth had
the blackest complexion,
did you not know,
your black is a blessing?

Did you not know,
you black is extravagant?
Multifaceted and talented,
you are history, in motion,
black excellence.

Not just athletes and activist,
kings and queens, spiritual beings,
Did you not know your
black is immaculate?

Although every shade
ever made has soul.
Did you not know,
your black is gold?

The universe made you
from the ashes of heaven.
Sing it loud and proud.

MY BLACK IS A BLESSING
MY BLACK IS A BLESSING
MY BLACK IS A BLESSING.

Self-Love Is The Best Love

I hope one day
you'll realize all
the love that you're
looking to find,
already exists within,
you just haven't
tookin' the time,
to see past the pain in
your reflections and try
looking inside.

Self love is the best love
you just have to be
willing to put in the time.

Maybe you're
feeling the pain
because things aren't
really the same,
but how do you expect to
do better if you're not
willing to change.

Embrace all of
your feelings,
and stop living in
self-pity and shame.

Sometimes the sun dies
and even sunflowers
have to sit in the rain.

The Laws Of Love

The more you
avoid self-love,
the more the
universe will
send you people
who don't know
how to love you.

The cosmos is
wrapped in its
own love,
the universe
inside you
deserves
love too.

Eleda Read

Why do you spend
all of this energy
looking for love
when you already
possess it?

Enough love to
light up the
streets of heaven
and make Jesus,
Allah, and Buddha
blush in your presence.

You have to
realize your worth
before you give it away,
otherwise you'll
give it to someone
who deserves
minimum wage.

Oceans *changing relationships*

You never really
learned to love yourself
and that's why you
feel worthless within,
and for this exact
same reason you're
willing to let that
person hurt you again.

Expecting love in all the
wrong places, so impatient
as the searching begins,
but you'll never find
sunshine until you
open the curtains within.

You hurt and pretend,
time and time again,
but things really
haven't been the same,
and every heartbreak
leaves you even more
broken, hoping that
their feelings change.

How many tears have
to trickle down your
window pane before
you realize that you
need to invest in you,
you do know that
sometimes the things
that hurt the worse
are what's best to do.

Nobody likes to
swim alone but its
more difficult when
you have to take
breaths for two.
In the ocean of life
when your love boat
sinks only you can
rescue you.

Reflections

I'm sorry they made you
hate your reflection.

So you hide it behind
make-up and mascara,
just to feel like you'll
make more progression.

In a world that's
so stuck up on
physical enhancements
and the media trying
re-design you.

But never let what's
behind you define you.
Real beauty is inside you.

Eventually

Don't spend all
of eternity looking
for someone to
have and to hold.

Though it may
seem irrational,
those who have
learned to love
themselves have
the happiest souls.

Maybe it's meant
for you to experience
yourself as one entity,
and then someone
comes along to
love you equally
eventually.

Better You

Some people become
heartbroken and
start living their
lives in reversal,
but never let
past situations
curse you to the
point you
start becoming
the person
who hurt you.

Heartbreak always
leaves a little residue,
but only pick up
the necessary
pieces to love
yourself and
become a better you.

Torn

A part of you
wants to go back
and the other half
wants to be alone,
but nobody but
you can heal your
pain so maybe
alone is where
you belong.

Heavy

If you're really
looking for love
you should
turn inside.

And if you decided
to let go you would
learn to fly.

Justice

Life poetic justice.
The more you get
hurt the more you
grow to love it.

But when you learn
to love yourself
you can climb
any height.

And every moment
will feel like the
time of your life.

Saved

People will always express
that they never meant to,
after they hurt you, but
their actions will always
prove they had the intent to.

And that makes you question
everything that you've
ever been through, has any-
thing they ever said been true,
how many times have they
ever went against you,
when the relationship went bad
who did they vent to?
These are the questions you
ask yourself when it hits you.

And then you start to feel
resentful, because you know
you've always been faithful
and eventually you will break
up but never let it break you,
just pray and be grateful, the
universe has saved you.

Strange

You never see caterpillars
making love to butterflies

For Once

Maybe for once you
should try loving you,
before you cake up
and wake up with
another dude.

…..Few months
later he tries to
cut you loose
and start looking
for another you.

The Dive

The only medicine
for loneliness is
being alone.

The strong become
best friends with
solitude and for
this reason alone,
they learn to be
on their own.

Within the pools
of your emptiness
there are stones and
shimmering jewels,
that can only be
found when you
dive deep into
yourself and
experience you.

True

When you were
 younger, your
greatest wish was
to be in love when
you grew up.

Heartbroken.
Time healed.

Feelings lost,
but finding
True love.

They never
told you:
You never
knew love,
until you
grew love.

That is
True love.

Practicing Self-Love

What is self-love

I often get emails and messages on social media from individuals inquiring as to what exactly is self-love and how to practice it. It really doesn't surprise me, although maybe it should, seeing as though our culture is so focused on what is on the outside that even the idea of loving yourself seems somewhat foreign and unknown.

For the most part, and from a very early age, we are mostly taught things from a materialistic or an "other focused" point of view. We are influenced to do things like go to school, get an education, get a job, make money, find a husband or wife, travel, and a wide range of other things that are supposed to help us be successful and happy in life.

Although these things are essential to our advancement in life, they are not as important as our parents, family, teachers, and mentors telling us to "LOVE YOURSELF" or even mentioning what self-love is. Apart from not being influenced to self-love, in western culture we are not properly educated on the all-important knowledge of self. So, before we learn how to self-love, let us first understand exactly who this self is that we are loving.

Do you know who you are? When asked this question, most of us would answer with confidence, "Yes, I do!" We may go on and say our name and ethnicity, such as I'm American, African-American, Brazilian, Chinese, etc. In truth, these things actually hint to *what* we are, but have no affiliation to our real identity and *who* we are.

The first step in self-love is knowing and understanding that who you are is eternal spirit-soul; you are not this body. To help us understand better, let's take a look at your shirt. Yes, really; look at your shirt. Whose shirt is this? You probably answered, "This is my shirt" or something to that effect, showing that you are in possession of the shirt that you are wearing. It would be fair to say that you know you are not your shirt; so let's take it a step further. Take a look at your hand, legs, arms, fingers, etc. Whose body is this? Again, you may have said "this is my body" and you are correct in doing so, proving that you are neither your shirt nor your body, but you, your-self (spirit-soul) is in possession of these things.

Now that we have established that we are not this body and that our self is actually spirit-soul, let us begin to understand a deeper meaning of what love is.

Love is spiritual: it is an energy so powerful that it created our very existence in this world. Love too, is eternal, ever giving, full of compassion, and gratitude. Love is the most healing thing you will ever experience in this life and beyond; it is the very essence of life and what we all are searching for. Love is the driving force of man because it is the source from which we have manifested from. Finally, love is all about service. It is willing to not only invest, but also sacrifice time, energy, and life force for the total fulfillment of its object. Having identified both "self" and "love" as spiritual aspects of our existence, we can conclude that:

Self-Love is a spiritual practice in which one invests time, energy, and collective life force toward the total fulfillment of self.

How to self-love

B efore we get into how to self-love, I'd like to revisit my personal definition/explanation of the practice and also give an elaborate commentary on the subject.

Self-Love is a spiritual practice in which one invests time, energy, and collective life force towards the total fulfillment of self.

Why is Self-Love spiritual? You are a divine being; the very fabric of your existence is timeless, blissful, radiant, and spotless. Everything about you is spiritual! Anytime we give a description or attributions of the "self" we are referring to a person's soul and real identity. This is the source of life within us, the force that gives us purpose and light that leads us into eternal sunshine. The practice of self-love is spiritual because you are, in fact, spiritual!

When did it begin? When we enter into this world as children, we are full of so much life, happiness, curiosity, innocence, and bliss. All of these things come natural to us. Aside from being fed and cared for, we are pretty much un-reliant on people to make us happy, as we seem to be completely self-fulfilled. And, actually, we are.

I like to use the analogy of a full cup of water. In our early years of life this is what we are, totally self-fulfilled, full in self as a full cup of water if you will. We are comfortable with who we are and we express that in every way we know how to. We jump, play, scream, shout, laugh, and smile, sometimes for no apparent reason at all. We love and embrace everything we are in our small world.

As we get older, people start telling us what we can, can't, and shouldn't do. They may call us names, yell at us, make us cry, and do things that hurt us. These things make us feel ashamed to be and to embrace everything that we naturally are. On top of this, sometimes we are given false identities. We are told things like, "you're shy," "you're not smart," "you have problems," etc. All of these things are what they perceive us to be but pretty soon we start to believe them and in some cases we start to embrace these identities, becoming the very things they call us.

Therefore, we have now been given a false identity or a misrepresentation of self and that full cup that we once had is now emptied little by little as time progresses.

The Saga Continues: As we reach our adolescent years and into adult-hood, we get into dating and building relationships with the opposite sex and things really start to get rocky.

Due to our childhood, we come into relationships unknowing and unfulfilled with who we are and the cup that was once filled with natural happiness and joy is now a bit more depleted. At this point, we start to look towards others to make us feel happy and to fill the cup back up. This is a big mistake. Actually, no one can make us happy; they can only add to the happiness that we already have within ourselves.

Once we have the mindset that someone can make us happy, we give him or her the power to make us unhappy as well. "We attract who and what we are." This is one of the most important secrets within all relationships and the best way to indicate if you've been treating yourself well. If we haven't been actively practicing self-love and aren't too satisfied with who we are, it's more than likely the partner we have "chosen" deals with the same issues of self-fulfillment and happiness as we do.

Now, both individuals involved are looking towards the other person to make them feel a sense of worth and happiness. Pretty soon, the fulfillment that we thought we would find in the other person is not there. Regardless of how much sex you have, how many gifts you exchange, or things you do, there will always be this feeling of emptiness inside of you and a desire you can't explain. The cup is a bit emptier.

Is it really love? For many, this is the point where our perception and understanding of love really starts to become distorted.

When desire goes unmet and happiness goes unfulfilled, we tend to become angry with ourselves. In fury, one partner may lash out, make selfish decisions, ending up doing and saying things that hurt the other. All of this because one is not making them happy or fulfilling their desires, a job that in their eyes their partner was supposed to do, but failed at. Although this task wasn't theirs to begin with, one is held accountable for not satisfying the other in their hunger for complete fulfillment.

This can work either way, with males or females, but usually what happens next is an onslaught of lies, arguments, and sometimes even cheating.

When a person acts selfishly for their benefit only, it is not love, it is a form of lust. Lust says, "forget my partner's feelings, I want to satisfy my needs, regardless of how much it may hurt them." This hurt may drain us or make us feel unworthy of true love and, again, the cup is emptied a bit more.

I have nothing left in me: From the time of our first heartbreak, or well before, depending on our upbringing, love tends to take on a different meaning each time we get involved with someone.

It used to seem so fun, care-free, kind, and exciting. Now love is more like a job. We are getting older and it's like we are supposed to have it and be in it by now. But, at this point, we've been in and out of several relationships, hurt over and over again, and still haven't healed or spent time refilling our cups.

That sense of self-fulfillment and happiness we possessed as a child seems to evade us in every moment of our lives and we spend most of our adulthood trying to figure out how to regain it. Again, we usually attract what we are, ending up being with someone who doesn't know the true meaning of love, and are not fulfilled within themselves either.

By the end of several episodes of "love," you're drained and have nothing left in you; you've come to think you may never experience the love you've always imagined. It's almost as if the universe doesn't want you to be in love. This is not true at all, but there is deeper reasoning.

I've been quoted saying, "As long as you keep avoiding self-love, the universe will keep sending you people who don't know how to love you." This is one of life's greatest lessons and the solution to all of your troubles in love.

Let's get to it: Self-love first starts with the commitment to put yourself first. You've spent too much time and effort pouring love into others; it's time to fill your own cup. Those who may be empathetic, the healers or the givers in a relationship, may have the most difficult time making this commitment because they're so focused on others as they don't want to let anyone down.

It's important for us to understand that self-love is not selfishness. Rather, it's recognizing that, "If I'm not totally happy and fulfilled in myself then it's likely that no one I meet will be happy and satisfied within themselves. I am willing to make this sacrifice for me, to ensure that all of my relationships are healthy and fulfilling."

Once we make this self-declaration, there is no turning back to our old ways of thinking and we have now taken our first step on the path of self-love.

The next thing we need to do is remove ourselves from all toxic situations and toxic people. Influence is everything and right now you don't need any negative or hurtful people around you draining you, distracting you from your practice. Although it is possible and important to self-love while in a relationship, now is not the time, as much of all of your focus needs to be on you.

Sometimes it may be hard to let go or shake toxic situations. This is normal as negative energy is very strong. As long as it has your attention, it will lure you back in and give you the illusion that this is what's best for you. I guarantee you it's not and until you break all ties with this energy you will continue to be hurt time after time, until you learn it's just not for you right now.

What completes you? True happiness comes from being totally satisfied and fulfilled within self. Now that we have made a commitment to ourselves and we have dropped all the baggage weighing us down, we are ready to start filling that cup back up!

We all come from the same source–God–and there are six attributes of our creator that relate to our desires of total fulfillment in life. What makes God, God, is that He possesses all knowledge, all strength, all beauty, all fame, all renunciation, and all wealth. Again, because we come from this source, all of our desires coincide with these six attributes and lead to being fulfilled in our life.

Although it's impossible for us to become or be God, possessing all of these characteristics in full, by practicing the following self-love practice, we can reach great amounts of happiness, self-fulfillment, and finally learn to love ourselves. I'd also like to add that I have practiced this myself for over two years now and I guarantee its effectiveness, as it will make you happier, more blissful in nature, and radiant with love for self and others.

The actual practice: Are you ready? In my practice, I like to refer to them as the "Self-Love Six." These are the six practices that are the very embodiment of self-love, the how to, and, if practiced consistently, the way to fill your cup.

Each of the six areas of practice are labeled below, along with a brief explanation, and a few personal suggestions. I recommend that, if you are serious about your self-love practice, you purchase or make a journal of sorts to track your progress and log your daily routine. Although some of your practices may overlap in other areas at times, they should be done alone. You may not like the idea of doing so, but it is essential that you spend as much time doing these things on your own as possible.

Why you may ask? Because it is in solitude that you will get to experience the most of your being and hear the song of your soul. Every soul sings a song. In which the story of our lives can be heard, and If you are in sync with this song, life will begin to unfold in the most beautiful and poetic fashion. When we add others to the equation, it's very hard to hear that song, because we now have to entertain their needs, thoughts, and desires. If the individual is not in tune with themselves and their own personal song, then the "mixing of melodies" are sure to cause an arrhythmic tune.

Solitude is one of the greatest tools when you're needing to find the answers to your life's problems or to rediscover yourself. If you are one of those people that can't bear to be alone, then this practice will be challenging in the beginning, but with constant effort and determination, you will feel so comfortable in your own energy that you won't feel a desperate need to have others around to enjoy yourself. But don't worry, your self-love practice does include others, and as you learn to balance yourself, it will allow you to better choose others who are of benefit to your practice.

Spiritual: Our Creator is the perfect renunciant. Renunciation in relation to our self-love practice is in terms of nonattachment. One of the first lessons we must undergo in learning to love ourselves more, is to learn and master the art detachment. At times it is our attachment to people, things, thoughts, habits and lifestyles that stop us from growing and embracing ourselves. Attachment also causes you identify yourself with things that are not you, or it may even cause you to lose yourself in the identity of others. Some of us give our complete souls to the objects of our friendship and love, leaving ourselves totally clueless to who we are or what makes us happy after the relationship has run its course. Your soul belongs to God, and you should never give that much of yourself to anyone. After we have given so much of ourselves away, it's imperative that we embrace, reclaim and rediscover who we are, and our spiritual practice allows us to do so.

Again, you are a spiritual being. You will always feel incomplete, unfulfilled, and dissatisfied with life when you don't have a particular spiritual regimen that you follow. When we practice self-love, we are in actuality, fulfilling the purpose of all living creation.

There is only one true Self, and that is God. Before time began, before the stars gathered, and the sun and moon danced among them, before roses of planets hung from the vines of creation, before the celestial ball commenced, and man found himself front and center on the stage of life, there was God. He was blissfully alone, singing to Himself, the most enchanting vibration known to His own existence. He then felt, I am alone, I am bliss, but I have no one to experience this bliss that I am, nor hear this song that I sing. And lo! Just as he thought, creation sprang forth! The one Eternal Spirit manifested Himself into many souls so that they may enjoy Him, the only true Self. We were created for no other reason but to know and love God, and thus by loving yourself you are simultaneously loving Him. God smiles when you love yourself. The more you practice experiencing yourself, you will be drawn closer to experiencing and knowing God. This is known by personal experience.

Because we are spiritual beings, and this is a spiritual practice, we need to designate days and times to focus on developing, nurturing, and fulfilling our spiritual nature. We have this propensity or desire within us to express our spirituality in some way, but often this gets put on the back burner because we may not think it's important or we may just not know how to do this.

The practice of spirituality doesn't always mean attending church or temple services; rather, it can be expressed daily in various ways. I can also include anything from yoga, meditation, japa, reading scriptures/daily devotionals, listening to sermons or religious commentary, praying, writing positive affirmations, or spending quiet time in nature alone. (no phones, no music, no technology, just listen). All of these things are spiritual practices that can be done daily.

Find time each day, if not once a week, to do any of the above-mentioned practices and write down your experience in your personal journal.

Artistic: God possesses all beauty and we also have this desire to do so as well. Real beauty has nothing to do with our physical appearance; it is within us and it expresses itself in the physical form. God expresses Her beauty in creation; everything from human life, to plants, oceans, mountains, sunsets, and waterfalls is an artistic expression of Her beauty. This is where our desire to express beauty and create comes from, and we must fulfill this desire in some way.

Many may say they don't have any artistic talents or abilities, but I can assure you we all have been blessed with this ability to create and express ourselves artistically. Your artistic practice can be expressed through drawing, painting, dancing, singing, writing poetry, screenplay writing, photography, videography, acting, modeling, graphic design, arts and crafts, building or assembling things, performing, or simply journaling your daily activities. Anything that allows you to create or express yourself is an artistic practice.

You will find your artistic practice to be one of the most healing practices amongst this list. When we create, we rid ourselves of all of the emotions, feelings, and thoughts that we have stored within. Creating allows us to express the beauty and sometimes the pain that is written on the walls of souls. That which must find a form of expression. I urge you to never deny your ability to create, for when you do, you deny your existence. You are here to create something special for the world to behold when you are no longer around, to leave an expression of your soul on earth so that others may be inspired to live, dream, and embrace themselves.

One of the things that I've done that has help me be the creative spirit that I am, was to seek a void that I wished to see fulfilled in society as a whole. In others words I've always been inspired to be the change that I wanted to see, or in this case, create what I thought needed to be created. I live by this method. If my favorite creators are not speaking about the things I feel need to be talked about, or what I would enjoying hearing, then I take it upon myself to create it. If you feel that there are things in the world that you wish to see created, but are not, you have found your purpose without a doubt. It is your job to create it!

Find time each day, if not once a week, to do any of the above-mentioned practices and write down your experience in your personal journal.

Educational: We have a desire to know things because our creator is all-knowing and full of wisdom. To fulfill this desire and void in our existence, we must be adamant about the cultivation of knowledge.

Knowledge can be acquired by reading, listening to lectures, or watching informative broadcast or documentaries. It doesn't always have to include learning hard issues like history, politics, economics, etc., but you can venture into fun facts, sports, or anything that peaks your interest. What's important is that you try to learn something new and exciting every day.

When we learn new things, we expand our minds and broaden our levels of perception, thus allowing us to welcome all that the universe has to offer in its vastness.

Find time each day, if not once a week, to do any of the above-mentioned practices and write down your experience in your personal journal.

Financial: Why does everyone seek wealth? It is because our Creator is abundantly infinite. He fashions starlit galaxies around his celestial body, his crown is adorned a million diamond like sun's, his heavenly abode is made of crystals of divine light, and He travels instantly at the speed of mind! There is no one who can say that they possess more wealth than God, for He is the sole creator of it, and it is His energy. Wealth and money alone does not equate to happiness, but it does give us a certain amount of freedom to do what we love and experience more of life. It is also a tool needed to help us in all areas of our self-love practice.

Our financial practice can include our job or career, creating weekly/monthly financial budgets, managing our bank account, saving money daily, reading financial reports or books on financial development, taking classes dealing with economics, or attending seminars on wealth empowerment.

As with all practices, this should not be your main focus, as it's all about finding the perfect balance to fulfill the propensity we have within us.

Find time each day, if not once a week, to do any of the above-mentioned practices and write down your experience in your personal journal.

Physical: Physical activities help us to exude and express the power of will and strength that the Creator possesses and has blessed us with. When we fail to exercise our strength and

God given will, we tend to become lazy, stagnant, or unproductive. Also, because we are experiencing a physical world, it's important that we keep our physical bodies in shape and active so that we may live a life of good health and longevity. Physical activities also help relieve stress and take our mind off the everyday troubles of the world, providing us with an outlet to let go and express some of the excess energy that we have stored within. There are days and sometimes weeks, when I spend too much time writing and creating, that I come to find myself lacking inspiration or focus, and need to take a break to do something active. Most times when I do, I return to my work much more in tune with my thoughts and inspired to create because I have given the energy stored from sitting and thinking all day, a physical outlet.

Activities can include, but are not limited to, walking, running, jogging, yoga, weight lifting, dancing, ballet, playing basketball, soccer, footfall, or tennis.

Find time each day, if not once a week, to do any of the above-mentioned practices and write down your experience in your personal journal.

Social: Who is more famous than God? Though He is known by many names, everyone has heard and knows of Him. He is famous because He exist in every being and in every ounce of creation. We seek to be known and commune with others because our Source can secretly be found behind familiar or intriguing faces. It is God who speaks through the poet, sage, and the saint. It is God who loves through the mother and father, and comforts as a friend you when you are in need of someone to talk to. It is God who is the voice behind melodies that uplift your spirit. God is the Lover behind all lovers, the Face behind all faces, and the Soul behind all souls. Everyone we meet gives us an opportunity to love and express our appreciation to God. We were made to be social creatures for this reason alone. To add, there's only so much alone time one can take, as we all have a desire to be in the company of others, and our social activities provide us the opportunity to do so.

After a long day/week of studying, working, creating, learning, and exercising, it's good to reconnect with our friends, family, partners, or even meet new people. Anything that allows you to speak and communicate with someone other than yourself is considered a social activity.

Your social activity may overlap with the other five areas of practice, i.e. Attending church or going to the gym with a friend constitutes as both a social and a physical activity.

Find time each day, if not once a week, to do any social activity and write down your experience in your personal journal.

What's Next: All that's left now for you to do is to put these practices into action! Imagine giving yourself all the love that you wish you had received in a relationship and remember that you attract who and what you are.

If you really want to see a change in your life and become more self-loving, you will. But, it requires a full investment of your time and energy. I advise you to set designated times to focus on each area specifically and be adamant about it. Once you have created your self-love plan, it is important to ask yourself, "What could possibly get in the way?" Once you have figured out what obstacles you may encounter, focus on what you can do to remove these barriers and if you can't remove them, you might want to adjust your strategies to make them more helpful to your practice. It can be challenging if your workplace or home is not supportive of self-love activities, but you can still do things outside of them to help yourself in your practices. It is important that your plan resonates for you and that you put it into action.

Maybe you're not ready now, but there will come a time when you will have to sit down with yourself and work out within you, all that needs to be healed. Until you make the decision to do so, your "inner chaos" will be reflected in every friendship, relationship, and every endeavor you pursue. It's best that you choose today, to begin the self -work and healing process that needs to take place. When you decide to transform yourself from the inside out, you not only become a better person, but you also allow better relationships to form in your life.

The beauty of practicing self-love is that you are always discovering new things about yourself. It's a truly adventurous journey and a constant unfolding of who you are, and if you dare to venture deep enough, it will reveal to you many wondrous things about life itself. Again, this is the very practice I use daily and, for me, it has been the most fulfilling thing, outside of finding God, that I have ever experienced. I hope that it can do the same for you. Happy self-loving!

Every soul sings a song,
in which the story of
our lives can be heard

God smiles when
you love yourself.

The Joy of Continence
& Practicing Celibacy

I was very hesitant to add this brief section to this edition of the book due to the fact that, though I've been practicing celibacy and continence for over two years, I have fallen once in my commitment towards maintaining it. I have chosen not to emit my thoughts and commentary on the practice because it would be an injustice to those seeking more of themselves, not to hear of the power that it grants them. I am not perfect, but I do strive for perfection, as it is every man and woman's right to do so. Celibacy is a choice, deliberately made; a decision not to enter marriage. Simply being single does not make one celibate (or else even a young adult or child could say they were celibate), but instead, it means one has chosen to forgo the act of marriage for personal or spiritual reasons. We can remain celibate for as long as we like, be it a few months or years. The choice is completely ours to make. Continence is also a choice. It is the decision not to engage in sexual intercourse. As in celibacy, the element of choice is important because those who want to have sex but are not able to, are not practicing continence. For individuals who are truly wanting to learn to love themselves more, along with the practices mentioned in the previous section, the practice of continence and celibacy is the sure way to do so.

There is no greater bliss than the joy that is found in continence. I am happy because I am continent. I am much more focused and productive because I am continent. I feel freer than I have felt because I am continent. Continence is the key that opens the doors to total fulfillment and happiness in life. It is not only the key, but the driving force that will take you anywhere that you wish to go in life. The sex energy is the driving force in man and woman too. Without it we all would be pretty dull and have no true ambition in life. Though we may not admit it, it is the sex attraction and urge that is the fire behind all of our endeavors. Men work hard to achieve their goals, in hopes to impress and attract a beautiful wife or mate. Women too, though they are more discreet, are driven by sexual energy. They also work to fulfill their desires, and also endeavor to be striking enough to attract a male to engage with and start a family.

There is no denying the presence of the sexual influence in all that we do and aspire to do. Indeed, there is no harm in acknowledging its existence in our minds and being, but there is much to be lost when we choose to act in a wrong manner towards its powerful influence.

God has given us sexual energy so that we may use it to maintain this earthly kingdom and also attain His kingdom in heaven. Sex energy is the fuel of gods; those who do not waste or overuse this energy are the most ambitious, right thinking, and creative individuals that walk this planet. If sex and the sex energy have the power to create life, imagine the power that one would possess in retaining it. If you wish to be a master of your craft, overflowing with creativity, and God-inspired genius, then the practice of continence is one of the many great secrets. Since beginning my own practice, I have noticed wondrous amounts of creative inspiration that strikes down like a bolt of lightning out of the ether into the soil of my consciousness, filling my mind with jolts of enlightenment, beautiful poetry, and creative ideas. There are some days that I awake out of sleep with entire poems ready to be recorded on paper from the "Messenger" of my mind. It's truly unexplainable, but I know it would not be possible without the continued practice of continence.

Continence is the pinnacle practice if you are looking to become more peaceful, happy, and glow with a universal love for yourself and all others. If you truly wish to know God and the ways of the universe, then there is no other way to know and become enlightened than to abstain from the over indulgence and attachment to sex. The universe pours grace into the continent and celibate being, allowing him or her the freedom to dive into its ocean of immaculate bliss, swim in its mysterious depths, and uncover the gems of wisdom and knowledge that are hidden from the vast majority of individuals. A great number of the world's phenomenal masters, saints, creatives, geniuses, and inventors have realized the power of sexual energy and have used it to transform themselves and change the world. Jesus Christ, Mother Teresa, Joan of Arc, Nikola Tesla, Isaac Newton, Andy Warhol, Plato, Aristotle, Beethoven, and many other men and women who have transformed the world, have practiced either continence or celibacy throughout their lives.

Continence not only comes with many spiritual benefits, but also a great number of physical and psychological benefits as well. There is no greater joy than the bliss that continence brings! It's like breathing for the first time, inhaling the scent of your soul's flowers, and exhaling the pure love and ecstasy of your spirit. Having no sexual attachment to the bodies of others frees your mind from a ton of unnecessary stress and worry caused by being involved with someone sexually. When we overindulge in sex we become lazy and lack the drive to do anything productive with ourselves. Having sex also causes us to become attached to people, which leads to anxiety, depression, and other psychological maladies. When we open ourselves up to another person sexually we give our most vital energy to them, making a connection with them in mind, body, and spirit. A piece of us is now occupying them and vice versa. Our judgment becomes cloudy and sometimes we find ourselves not behaving or acting in ways that we are not familiar with.

Sex is the exchange and sharing of energy. Though our physical bodies appear to be solid matter, they are composed of what is called life energy or *prana*. This life energy is vibrating at high speeds and makes the body and other physical objects appear as concrete. When we have sex, we mix our energy with others and whatever tendencies and habits they may have, if we are not aware of it, we can also take them on. In most of my relationships in the past I found myself the victim of the exchange of this unwanted energy caused by engaging in sex. I would feel depressed for no reason at all, I would say and do things that were not of my nature, and I always felt the need for reassurance even though I had no reason to be insecure. I had not only become a slave to the sex desire but also a slave to the effects that it had on the mind. Sex causes bondage. To abstain is to attain total freedom in mind, body, and spirit.

I speak with confidence on the topic now, but in the beginning it was not easy at all. Being a heterosexual male I found it difficult to escape the sexual urge. Everywhere I looked there it was, SEX. On the T.V., in movies, on social media, in the news, in art, in music; it was everywhere I turned. Sometimes I became so frustrated that I would do nothing but sit and write prayers for the urge and its reminders to go away, but they never did—and still haven't. I have yet to master myself enough to totally attain the level in purity in mind that I wish to have, but I have managed to be watchful and not entertain the sexual desires that come and go from it. As mentioned before, I have fallen in my practice, but I have learned from that experience that I have to be persistent in my will and mindful of the environments a allow myself to dwell in.

It takes an extreme amount of willpower to conquer the urge to have sex, as it is the force that drives us and allows us to reach anything worth attaining in life. It takes will to do everything; we use will to lift the fork that brings food to our mouths, we use it to write, dance, or sing, everything is executed by the usage of will. Will gives us the power to act and manifest things in our life. The more will you exert, the greater your chances are to accomplish the task. For this reason, I have found it unnecessary to try to conquer the sex desire, but by willpower, convert and transfer the energy into other areas of my life. Before taking this approach to sex, I felt as though I was simply suppressing the desire, which in turn caused me to become frustrated and agitated with myself. But when I learned the science and power that it instilled within me, I began to reap the benefits of its practice.

Again, there is no greater joy felt than the bliss experienced in the practice of continence. It is the apex of your journey into self-love and if you would allow yourself to taste a drop of this sweet joy you will come to know a happiness that you have never felt. The continent can achieve anything, create anything, and be anything, because they possess the will to control and master the greatest force with them. Thus, what is there in the world that they should not possess the power to overcome or gain?

Though it may be very hard to practice continence while dating or in a relationship, I encourage you to talk to your partner and try your best to regulate the indulgence in sex. If you are single, I also advise that you take a personal vow of celibacy and continence for whatever time frame that you deem necessary. I hope that this brief section has made you more confident in your own practice and/or has influenced you to be filled with all that it will bring. In my journey, which has not been a walk in the park, I have found encouragement and inspiration in reading articles on the subject, which has led me to carry out my practice. I leave a few of my favorite quotes and a prayer that I read often in the following pages.

"By the establishment of continence, energy is gained. The chaste brain has tremendous energy and gigantic will-power. Without chastity there can be no spiritual strength. Continence gives wonderful control over mankind. The spiritual leaders of men have been very continent, and this is what gave them power."

-Swami Vivekananda

"When a man succeeds in the conservation of his sexual energy, his intellect reflects the image of Brahman(God), even as a glass gives a perfect image when its back is painted with mercury solution.
The man who carries this image of Brahman in his heart is able to accomplish everything—
he will succeed wonderfully in whatever action he engages himself."

-Sri Ramakrishna

"When you really see how much God loves you, there's no greater love than that, and I had to match that amount of love He had for me, which is the reason why I decided to take a vow of celibacy."

-Jessica White

"I've tried everything but celibacy, and I really want to know what it feels like to be touched by someone with a mental touch and not a physical touch."

-LisaRaye McCoy-Misick

"During sex excitement, the best way to transmute sex impulses is to inhale and exhale deeply. Inhaling and exhaling withdraws energy from all parts of the body, especially the sex region, and concentrates it in the heart and lungs.

While inhaling and exhaling, the mind should be kept busy affirming: "I want to transmute sex energy into spiritual energy. I want to turn it God-ward to spiritually create." Through this affirmation, the brain becomes a spiritual magnet, pulling the transmuted energy from the heart and lungs into the spiritual cerebral reservoir.

Immediately after the sex impulse disappears, one should meditate or read a passage of Scripture. One can also engage the mind in creative, inventive, business, or literary work—whatever you find most absorbing. The more you practice this technique, the more you will transmute the sex impulse and overcome sex temptation."

-Paramahansa Yogananda

A Prayer for Purity

O loving Lord of Compassion! The Soul of my soul, the Life of my life, the Mind of my mind, the Ear of my ears, Light of lights, Sun of suns! Give light and purity. Let me get established in physical and mental continence.

Let me be pure in thoughts, word and deed. Give me strength to control my senses and observe my practice in full faith and remembrance of you. Protect me from all sorts of temptations of this world. Let all my sense be ever engaged in Thy sweet service.

Wipe out the sexual impressions from my mind and eliminate all subtle desires that linger in my subconscious. Annihilate lust from my mind. Let me be chaste in my look. Let me always walk in the path of righteousness.

Forgive all my offenses. I am Thine. I am Thine.
Enlighten, enlighten. Guide, protect.
Om Aum Amen.

Affirmations

"Words saturated with sincerity, conviction, faith, and intuition are like highly explosive vibration bombs, which, when set off, shatter the rocks of difficulties and create the change desired. Sincere words or affirmations repeated understandingly, feelingly, and willingly are sure to move the Omnipresent Cosmic Vibratory Force to render aid in your difficulty. Appeal to that Power with infinite confidence, casting out all doubt; otherwise the arrow of your attention will be deflected from its mark."

— Paramahansa Yogananda

Root Chakra Affirmations: Center Of Grounding, Safety, And Health

I am grounded in my own nature.
I feel safe with myself and my surroundings.
I am comfortable with being myself.
I love myself perfectly and I am perfectly healthy.
Every day I am getting healthier and healthier.
I am feeling better and better.
Every cell in my body is health conscious.
I am full of energy and vitality.
My mind is peaceful, serene, and calm.
I eat healthy foods that benefit my body.
I always feel good and as a result my body feels good.
Every day is full of hope, happiness, and health.
I have a right to be healthy.
I bless my body daily and take good care of it.
Good health is next to Godliness; I am divine.
I am in possession of a healthy mind and body.

I am one with myself and all things around me.
I feel my natural connection to Mother Earth.
I treat my body as a temple; it is holy and full of goodness.
I release all ill feelings in me about people.
I forgive everyone associated with me.
I express my deep gratitude to God and everyone in my life.
I am aware that I am incomplete without you all.
"Healthy, wealthy, and wise" is my mantra.
My body is healthy.
I am wealthy in spirit.
My mind is ever wise.
I am healthy because I say I AM.
I AM
So be it.

Sacral Chakra Affirmations: Center Of Creativity, Sexuality, And Expression

I feel great about myself.

I want the best for myself.

I feel all things are working for my good.

I feel God's presence in my life.

I express myself in a healthy way.

I express my innermost feelings in a healthy way.

I express my emotions to those that I love.

I am an expression of God's love.

In my life I choose happiness and abundance.

Pleasure is a sacred aspect of my life.

I trust the process of life and I am open to all experiences.

My body is a sacred vessel and I treat it with honor and respect.

My sexuality is sacred. I embrace my sensuality and my sexuality.

I trust my intuition and allow it to guide me.

My life is full of grace and self-pleasure.

I allow my emotions to flow through my body in a healthy way.

I am open to the magic of the universe.

The universe is full of eternal abundance.

I am grateful for the joy of being me.

I receive pleasure and abundance in every breath.

When I create, it enriches my spirit and brings me bliss.

My desires are balanced.

I am joyful, spontaneous, and creative.

My body responds to the thoughts of pure love and goodness.

Nobody needs to heal me or complete me.

I reclaim my personal power to look after myself.

As I love and respect myself, healing and growth happens naturally.

I love and enjoy my body.

I have healthy values and boundaries.

My sexuality is sacred.

I realize that my emotions are the language of my soul.

I let go and release all things that prohibit my spiritual growth.

I am divine.

I am expressive.

I am creative.

I am at peace.

Solar Plexus Affirmations: Center Of Willpower, Confidence, And Self-esteem

I act only in ways that benefit me spiritually.

I am free to do and act as my soul guides me.

I love and accept myself fully.

I choose happiness in all areas of my life.

I am confident in my abilities.

I am able to do all that I put my mind into.

I am working in cooperative efforts with the universe.

I am happy, I am peaceful, I am joyous.

I am disciplined in all areas of my life.

I choose situations that allow me to grow spiritually.

I face all challenges in life with an open mind.

All challenges make me spiritually stronger.

I choose to be all that I can be.

I choose to accept the path God has given me.

I have the power to choose what's best for me.

I invest in myself every day.

I appreciate my life.

I give thanks and gratitude for all things in my life.

I am confident in myself.

I am confident in my talents.

I am confident in my gifts.

I am confident in my goals.

I place all of my confidence in God.

The universe supports me in all of my endeavors.

I act with kindness.

I act with respect.

I act with love.

I am confident in my actions.

I am strong and fearless.

I can overcome all that I am faced with.

I am Divinely guided and protected.

My life is full of spiritual growth.

I am at peace.

Heart Chakra Affirmations: Center Of Love, Compassion, And Joy

I love and accept myself unconditionally.
I love everything about my life.
I love my connection to God and all things.
I am compassionate.
I am caring.
I am giving.
I let go of all hurtful situations.
I forgive all things that have hurt me.
I am open to receiving divine love.
I am open to receiving universal love.
I am open to giving myself the love I wish to receive.
I see all things with loving eyes and I love all that I see.
To me, love is the only thing that exists.
I am compassionate towards all things that have life.
I am one with all things that have life.

I accept myself for who I am.
I am always growing in love.
I have the right to love myself and others.
I am open to receiving the love of others.
With love I can conquer all things.
By loving God first, I can do all things.
By loving myself first, I can receive the love I deserve.
Self-love is an important part of my spiritual growth.
Love is the center of my universe.
I do all things with a loving mind and heart.
I feel love all around me.
I radiate love and feel good about myself.
Of all things in life, love is most important.
I am careful of those I choose to share my most confidential love
with.
The person that I seek is also seeking me.
We will be brought together in divine love.
I am love.
I am loved.
I am at peace.

Throat Chakra: Center Of Communication And Truth

I speak spiritual growth into my life.

I speak abundance into my life.

I speak love into my life.

I speak divine guidance into all areas of my life.

I speak of only things that I want to grow in my life.

I communicate effectively with others.

I communicate with those that I love.

I communicate with those that I work with.

I communicate with God every chance I get.

I love to share my experience in spiritual growth with others.

I am open to listening to others.

I express my love of God.

I express my gratitude toward life.

I seek to always speak the truth.

I stand behind my words.

I know when to speak and when to listen.

I allow myself time to hear the wisdom of the universe.

I am pure in my actions, words, and deeds.

I realize that speech is sacred.

I speak only of things I would like to see manifest in my life.

I always speak the truth.

I speak wisdom into my life.

I speak blessings into my life.

I seek to understand all things of truth and wisdom.

I trust that I am Divinely guided and protected.

I am at peace.

Brow Chakra Affirmation: Center Of Understanding And Wisdom

I am connected with all things that have life.

I seek to understand life.

I seek to understand myself.

I seek to understand God.

I believe all things are possible.

I believe in myself.

I believe in my abilities.

I believe in the magic of believing.

I can because I believe I can.

I can do anything because I believe I can.

I ensure that all of my beliefs are positive.

I trust my intuition.

I see all things with clarity.

I see everything with eyes of love.

I am free from illusion.

I am open to receiving wisdom.

My awareness is ever expanding.
I trust in my higher self.
My spiritual vision is clear.
I see God in all things.
I see God in all people.
I am guided by my higher self.
I go with the flow of life.
I trust the process of life.
I am proud of my intellect.
I am self-aware.
I am clairvoyant.
I am full of imagination.
I use my imagination to help create my reality.
I have divine insight on my life.
I am open to inspiration.
I am intuitive.
I forgive so that I may grow.
I share my wisdom with others.
I am humble in my spiritual path.
I receive knowledge only from authorized sources.
I am aligned with the consciousness of the universe.
I am submerged completely in God consciousness.

Crown Chakra: Center Of Bliss, Happiness, And Peace

I am divine.

I am divinely guided.

I am open to divine consciousness.

I am full of bliss.

I am full of happiness.

I am eternally thankful.

I am eternally in the Lord's grace.

I am peaceful and protected.

I let go of all attachments in my life.

I allow myself to grow abundantly.

I am spirit soul.

I am not this body.

I am not this mind.

As I ascend I remind myself to stay grounded.

I ascend daily.

I am a being of divine light.

I see divine light in all things.

I am the embodiment of God's love.

I let go of my material attachments.

I choose the path of purity.

I am a sacred being.

I go beyond what I see and accept myself fully.

I have total trust in Spirit.

God is my source.

I serve God in all things I do.

I surrender the Divine creator of the universe.

My spirituality is sacred.

I develop my self-soul daily.

I choose the path of surrender.

All things are working for my highest good.

God is in control of my life.

Knowledge is mine.

Understanding is mine.

Love is mine.

Creativity is mine.

Wisdom is mine.

I feel deeply connected with my creator.

I feel deeply connected with all things.

The Source lives within me.

The seeds you sow,
have no choice but to grow.
Speak and think only of the things
you would like to see grow in the
garden of your life.

Cosmic Prayers

O Cosmic Ocean Pour Into Me

O cosmic ocean pour into me,
engulf me in the sea of your bliss,
wash away my impurities,
allow me to swim in thee, ever free.

O cosmic ocean pour into me,
fill me with your joy and grace,
shower me with your wisdom,
drown me in your Divine love.

As I calm the waves of my mind,
I see Thee ever clearer.
You are that diamond at the oceans floor.
My treasure, I draw ever near.

O cosmic ocean pour into me,
quench the thirst of my soul,
flood the rivers of my veins,
let your consciousness overflow.

I Wish To Play No More

Swinging on trees of life.
Spinning on wheels of karma.
Racing through reincarnations.
Jumping in sense enjoyment.
Catching pompous passions.
Falling in pits of pain.
Running in mazes of *maya*.
Chasing hills of fleeing fame.

Flying to you, God I soar.
I wish to play no more.

Reveal Thyself

O Mother Divine, reveal Thyself.
O Lord Jesus, reveal Thyself.
O Lord Krishna, reveal Thyself.
O Lord Buddha, reveal Thyself.
O Eternal Allah, reveal Thyself.
O Divine Self, reveal Thyself.

My Soul Blooms For You

I shall plant seeds of Thy joy in the garden my mind.
The soil, I fertilized with faith and water daily
through prayer and meditation.

Though many storms may pass, my gaze
is ever fixed on your eternal sunshine.
O Spirit, in the spring of my awakening,
my soul blooms for you.

Descend Upon Me

Christ, may your consciousness descend upon me.
May I love as you have loved.
May I forgive as you have forgiven.
May I speak as you have spoken.
May I do as you have done.
May I serve as you have served.
May I surrender as you have surrendered.
May I know as you have known.

For as many as received you, you have given
them the power to become sons of God.
In faith and complete surrender, I pray to Thee.
Christ, may your consciousness descend upon me.

Forever, I Am Thine

I am a vessel of your Divine love, pour into me thine
blessed grace, let Thy eternal fountain wisdom overflow.
Father, when I speak let it be you who speaks through me,
let all of my actions be in union with your Divine will,
for I am never the "doer" but merely an instrument
in your Divine hands. Let others not see me for this
bag of flesh and bones, but allow them witness your
radiant Light that shines through me.

Forever I am Thine, in service and surrender.

That Eastern Star

Gazing through the window of that single eye,
I search for that eastern star. O shining light of
Christ come to me, I forsake you no more.

My Temple Of Peace

Heavenly Spirit, make my temple a place of peace.
Let the walls of my soul be as soft as a summers cloud
and the ceilings of my mind be ever spotless.
I place you on the altar of my heart, and open the
doors of my kingdom to receive your infinite bliss.
Lord, make my temple a place of peace.

My Infinite God

I serve an infinite God,
I do not know of limitations.
When I ask for His grace,
it is given to me abundantly.
When I ask for His love,
It is given to me abundantly.
All that I ask and work for,
is given unto me abundantly,
for my God is an infinite God.

O Blessed Spirit Transform Me

Father I give my entire being unto Thee,
leaving no parts unclaimed by you.
May you use me in any way that you see fit.
Let my only desire be to serve thee in my
greatest capacity, and your every command
be done without doubt or questioning.

My mind is yours, may it always dwell upon Thee.
My heart is yours, may I seek your love eternally.
My words are yours, may they reflect your wisdom.
My actions are yours, may they be aligned with your will.
My intelligence is yours, may it be purified in Thee.
All that I am, I surrender unto you.
O Blessed Spirit, transform me.

Am I Not Thy Child?

My soul cries.
My heart yearns.
My spirit weeps.
My mind sorrows.
But you cometh not.
Am I not a child,
made in thine image?

O infinite One, my devotion is to Thee,
bless me with thy cosmic presence,
glance upon me with Thine lotus eyes,
wrap me in Thy undying arms.

Am I not Thy child?

Satisfy My Infant Soul

For many births you have pacified me.
Temporary satisfactions have come with
the taste of sense enjoyment, money, name,
fame and the fulfillment of mundane desires.

No more do I seek these things,
it is only the milk of your infinite
wisdom that will satisfy my infant soul.

May I Return To My Divine Nature

When the heavens said, "let there be light",
was it not my infinite soul that sprung forth
amidst the vibration of that cosmic commandment?

Father I beg of thee, left these veils. Allow me
to behold the light that I am and you are.
Dissipate this darkness, eradicate this ignorance,
liberate me from all delusion.

May I return my divine nature.

Awake In Thee

I was fast asleep, but now, awake in Thee.
I slumber no more, melting away the
fabric of this cosmic dream.

No more mourning moon cries.
In the dawn of my awakening,
I silently sail serenity skies,
lit by the soft salient sunrise.

Transcendent Father, behold!
I am awake in thee!

My God Is Greater

With watchful eyes I see evil on the rise,
mischievous smiles preying on my demise,
lust and greed are the devils disguise,
but this kingdom of mine allows no evil inside.

Temptation flee me, my God is greater.

More Of You

No amount of wealth, success,
or prosperity can satisfy my
souls desire to commune with Thee.

If I am to inherit all the diamonds
in your kingdom at the cost of
losing you, I shall seek it not.

Lord take away everything,
if it means more of you.

In My Fathers Hands

In your divine presence my spirit
melts like clay in the potter's hands,
mold me to your likening. Shape me,
transform me, renew me in your image.
Though strong in faith, I am,
my spirit is supple in your hands.

In The Eyes Of The Lord

May I build a temple in my heart
that is welcoming to all God's children.
May the spirit of my being transcend the
laws of duality and reveal the oneness
in all of creation.

Holy Father, may my love for you unite the
many and draw them closer to the One.
Our home is heaven, our nationality is spirit,
our nature is transcendental. Help us to realize
that we are manifestations of you. Infinite,
eternal, all knowing, cosmic bliss. We are
perfect in the eyes of the Lord.

The Ocean Has Become A Wave

The wave cannot become the ocean,
but the ocean can become the wave.
From that cosmic causal ocean
of consciousness I have drifted away.
On earthly shores my soul awaits,
to return to thy abyss of bliss.
Lord protect me, shield me, cover me
in your grace, let me return to you in
the same manner I was sent.

The Minds Drift Towards Thee

I pray to Thee for no other reason but
to commune with thee. O beloved
Mother of creation, I seek nothing other
than your love, when I come to your
altar, I come fully engaged in you, letting
my mind drift only towards Thee.

Seeking To Know Thee

Supreme One, I am not satisfied with simply
believing in Thee. Am I not made in thine image?
Should I believe based upon second hand teachings
told by those of dogmatic and materialistic natures?
Father this void in my soul can only be filled by directly
experiencing you. My heart wishes to know Thee to be
as "real" as the pictures of light that you have casted
upon the shadows of the cosmos.

Ancient Father of mine, I wish to know and
experience Thee in truth, for there is no need
to believe when one has come to know the
object of his thoughts to be concrete.

A Treasure In God

No longer do I search for happiness
without, for I have found it within.
Men dig for diamonds, but I have
found a treasure in God.

Bathing In Eternal Rays

Teach me great One, to disassociate with
this ever changing body, and fix my deepest
concentration on the immortal changeless
spirit. I am a being of light, and thus, it is
not bread alone that supplies me with
life energy, but the cosmic vibration of
your Word. May it vitalize, energize and
recharge me.

I bathe in your eternal rays, soul-feasting on
your omnipresent cosmic energy that covers
and surrounds me in every moment. Father
God, starve my ego, feed spirit with more of you.

The Only Truth

O beloved Mother, I pray for the world, may they
find this peace and bliss that I have found in Thee.
May they relinquish all of their petty worldly desires
and make the ultimate sacrifice in finding you. For it is
only you, and you alone, that can bring peace and solace
into our weary spirits.

It is only your love that can heal and restore balance.
Mother of creation, bless your children that they may
have a desire to return home. We have abandoned
you in search of "something else", but success and
failure, joy and pain, wealth and poverty are but
dreams in this world. You are the only Reality.

Whispers Of Wisdom

I bathe my soul in silence, listening to Thy
sweet whispers of wisdom. In the ink of devotion,
with a watchful mind and persistent will, I write
your transcendental words on the pages of my heart.
Fill every line with your divine intelligence, let every
vibration stretch beyond the margins of my limited
perception and broaden my human consciousness.
O Author of Truth, inscribe upon my spirit your
universal message of love.

The Art Of Forgiveness

Many times I have abandoned Thee,
forsaken and denied thee, and yet
you embrace me with eyes of pardon.
O Giver of mercy, it is through you
that I have learned the art of forgiveness.

The Life Of All Lives

The tree of our lives will not bear fruit
if we do tend to its roots. You are the
Source and the Life that gives life to all.

I Wish To Reflect Your Loving Light

I place my deepest troubles and worries on the altar
of my heart. Father save me from the thoughts that
antagonize my mind, give me the strength to ward
off the negative impressions that hold the spirit captive.
My mind is muddy from the karma of past actions,
every step I take towards the summit of realization
seems futile, as my faithful grounds weaken beneath me.

A diamond that falls into a filthy place is still a diamond.
O oceanic Bliss, baptize me in you, I wish to reflect your
loving light once more.

Heaven Rescue My Spirit

The five beast of the body taunt and heckle me.
Heaven rescue my spirit from this jungle of temptation.

Dwell In Thee

Heavenly Spirit I ask humbly of you to remove all things
that may prohibit me from attaining you. Abolish these walls
of passion, cast out these obstacles of fear, anger, lust and greed.
Lift me beyond all desire for sense pleasure.
In Thee I wish to dwell eternally.

Seeing With Divine Eyes

For the eyes behold many beautiful temptations,
but greater is my desire to know their Source.

In The Hermitage Of My Heart

I offer my soul as a divine sacrifice to the consciousness
that is within and beyond creation. To that infinite One, I
pledge my allegiance to do Thy will as it is manifested
in me.

In the hermitage of my heart, I bow before thee in worship
and full surrender. May you come and bless this astral body
of light, that it reflects the radiance or your Divine Effulgence.
Infuse my causal body with cosmic thought that mirrors your
Supreme Consciousness. Interstellar Creator, may this body
be a church consecrated only for the Divine work.

Everlasting Life

I am not an old soul, I am ever new,
ever joyous, divinely infinite, existence itself.
At the turn dusk I fall, and resurrect at dawn.
For me, there is no birth, nor death, there is
only Life. Everlasting, ever new, unfolding, Life.

Dancing With Destiny

I dance with *maya* no more,
for I have at date with destiny.

Holding The Hands Of Heaven

The candle of my life is lit by that infinite Light,
guiding me on this inward journey.
Crossing cascades of confusion,
treading trails of temptation,
down dirt the roads of doubt,
across acres of anger,
passing pastures of passion,
leaping lakes of lust,
moving mountains of malice,
while holding the hands of Heaven.

With The Sword Of Will

With the sword of my will, I defeat the darkness of delusion and cast out these shallow shadows revealing myself as true light. I and my father are one, as infinite, undifferentiated, Cosmic Light.

Watered By The Word

From that one seed of eternal Sprit, innumerable souls were planted into the garden of creation. What shall water them but the Word; purified in perfection, Gods reflection, imbued with the Christ Consciousness, the only begotten of the Father.

My Hearts Sing's That Eternal Joy

In sadness my heart sings,
Hare Krishna, Hare Krishna,
Krishna Krishna, Hare Hare.
Hare Rama, Hare Rama,
Rama Rama, Hare Hare.

In sorrow my heart sings,
Hare Krishna, Hare Krishna,
Krishna Krishna, Hare Hare.
Hare Rama, Hare Rama,
Rama Rama, Hare Hare.

In success my heart sings,
Hare Krishna, Hare Krishna,
Krishna Krishna, Hare Hare.
Hare Rama, Hare Rama,
Rama Rama, Hare Hare.

In faith my heart sings,
Hare Krishna, Hare Krishna,
Krishna Krishna, Hare Hare.
Hare Rama, Hare Rama,
Rama Rama, Hare Hare.

In failure my heart sings,
Hare Krishna, Hare Krishna,
Krishna Krishna, Hare Hare.
Hare Rama, Hare Rama,
Rama Rama, Hare Hare.

In doubt my heart sings,
Hare Krishna, Hare Krishna,
Krishna Krishna, Hare Hare.
Hare Rama, Hare Rama,
Rama Rama, Hare Hare.

In devotion my heart sings,
Hare Krishna, Hare Krishna,
Krishna Krishna, Hare Hare.
Hare Rama, Hare Rama,
Rama Rama, Hare Hare.

In sadness, sorrow, success,
faith, failure, doubt, and
devotion, my heart sings
that eternal joy.

Free From The Money Taint

O giver of wealth, let my consciousness be above
and beyond the money taint. Worldly riches are
the instruments we are to use in service for the
divine work; it is your energy, and it flows from
your infinite being in abundance. Therefore allow
me to give freely without the attachment to its
possession and its rajasic and tamasic powers.

All that I gather shall be offered to you religiously,
for it is you who has allowed the fountains of grace
to water the seeds of wealth that have grown to
bear fruit in my life.

A Bouquet Of Souls

Beyond time and space, the Creator
awaits the return of His cosmic children.

I shall join thee soon, and bring with me
a bouquet of souls into Thy heavenly kingdom.

Awake In The Cosmic Dream

O this life is but a dream,
pictures of divine light
casted upon the shadows
of the cosmic screen.
Shouts and screams from
the audience of human beings,
nightmares recede as I bare
witness of the beam.

Awake in the cosmic dream.

I Come To Know Your Truth

Metaphysical Truth, I ask that you meet me
at my level of consciousness and bless me
with the gift of wisdom to understand truths
higher than my current perception. Thou art
infinite, and thus, the pond of my human mind
cannot conceive all of what dwells in the vast sea
of your intelligence. With a humble heart
and a seeking mind, I come to know your Truth.

The Seeker &
The Sage

Everything

The seeker:

Who am I?

The Sage:

You are literally
everything you
are looking for.
What are you
looking for?
You are
everything.
Literally.

The Soul

The seeker

What is the soul?

The sage:

You are not
the body
nor the mind.
The soul is what
you are, it is
neither born
nor does it die.
Free and
untouched
by impurities,
it is divine,
it is the lotus
in the sky.

Age

The seeker:

How old are you?

The sage:

What is age,
What is time,
I am here
I am now.
I am eternal
and you, too.
How new
are you?

Death

The seeker:

What happens
when we die?

The sage:

The caterpillar
has the same
soul as the
butterfly.

The seeker:

But the caterpillar
doesn't die.

The sage:

Yes, this is why.

Within Me

The seeker:

How is God
within me?

The sage:

When an apple
falls from a tree,
the tree is still
within the apple,
because of the seed.

Faith

The seeker:

How do I have
faith in the unseen,
how do I trust,
how do I believe?

The sage:

Strangers are not
trusted with gold,
we do not trust what
we do not know.
You must seek
to know God,
only then, in
faith you grow.

Doubt

The seeker:

I can't see Him,
how do I know
God is real?

The sage:

You speak much
of the soul.
Is this something
that you see,
or rather what
you feel?

Songs

The seeker:

I hear of many
gods, which is
right, which is
wrong?

The sage

In truth you will
find no wrongs,
listen closely and
you will hear only
different instruments
playing the same song.

God & Man

The seeker:
Is man, God?

The sage:

The wave and the
ocean are of the
same quality,
but not of the
same quantity.
Man, made in the
image of God,
is the drop of
water that flows
from the eternal
fountain of creation.

Here

The seeker:

What is the
purpose of life
and why are
we here?

The sage:

Some by choice,
and some by force.
The apple falls
from the tree
forgetting the
root as its source.

It may lay and decay
for days and weeks,
eventually returning
to mother's womb,
as she prepares it to be,
another amazing tree.

Peace

The seeker:

How do I
gain peace?

The Sage:

Peace is nothing
to be acquired.
You burn restless
because of desire.
Wishing to have
and gain more,
adds only to
the fire.

Misery

The seeker:

Is there any escaping
the misery of this world?

The sage:

What is pain
to the infinite soul,
in a world filled with
abundance you must
experience to grow.

Happiness & Bliss

The seeker:

How do I lead a
life of happiness?

The sage:

Happiness is this:
you, me, left, right
good, bad, pain, joy,
are all equal and bliss.
Everything is everything.

War

The seeker:

Why is there
war, why do
people rob
and kill?

The sage

Only as the dust
of illusion clears
will you come to
what is real,
as the heart
seeks light
does darkness
disappear.

Meditation

The seeker:

How do I meditate?

The sage:

Fix and train
your mind to
focus on the divine.
Chant within, the
names of God and
enter the sublime.
Hare Krsna
Amen
Aum
Om

The Path

The seeker:

How do I know
which path is
right for me?

The sage:

Walk the path
in front of you
without fear
nor hesitation,
in the circle
of life, all paths
eventually lead
to the same,
destination.

Heaven and Hell

The seeker:

Who gets into
heaven, who goes
to hell?

The sage:

The gates of heaven
are open to love,
that of all in creation,
and the Divine above.

There are many rest
stops in between,
but the gates of
hell are entered
through anger,
lust, and greed.

Free

The seeker:

How does one
become free?

The sage:

That is only a
state of mind,
in which you
wish to be.
You can build
walls or you
can grow
a garden.

The Return

The seeker:

When will
God return?

The sage:

Experienced in
every breath,
the taste of water,
when refreshed,
the syllable OM
that we express.
When has She
ever left?

And I am still learning.

Drawing ever closer God.
That Eternal Sunshine.

Tread as we all must.